Nikolai Dante

The Romanov Dynasty

RO... ...SER

Nikolai Dante pin-up by **Simon Davis**

NIKOLAI DANTE

Script: Robbie Morrison

Art: Simon Fraser

Colors: Simon Fraser, Alison Kirkpatrick

Letters: Annie Parkhouse

Originally published in *2000 AD* Progs 1035-1041

In the Year of the Tsar 2666 AD, Imperial Russia once again entered a time of troubles. The rule of Vladimir the Conqueror, Tsar of All the Russias, had been unopposed for centuries. Now it was being challenged by the House of Romanov, the most powerful Imperial Dynasty beside the Tsar's own.
Warfare on such a scale had not been contemplated since the Last Revolution, from which the Mafiya Clans rose to power. On the ashes of that conflict they founded a new Empire based upon the underworld principles of the ancient Vorovskoi Mir - The Thieves' World.
In such a world a single man could rise to prominence if he was a fool and an adventurer, a gambling man whose only stake was his life. Of course, this could only happen if he survived long enough and didn't get his throat slit in the boudoir of some Lady of dubious morals first...
SCRIPT
ROBBIE MORRISON
ART
SIMON FRASER
LETTERS
ANNIE PARKHOUSE

OHHH, DANTE!

TREACHEROUS SLUT!!
BOJEMOI!

AREN'T THE TSAR'S OWN HUSSARS PAYING ENOUGH FOR YOUR TALENTS AS AN IMPERIAL SEDUCTRESS, LADY ZOYA?
WHAT CAN I SAY? I JUST ENJOY MY WORK.

MEN! THIS ARROGANT YOUNG PUP'S TRYING TO TEACH OUR OLD DOG NEW TRICKS.
WE CAN'T ALLOW SUCH AN OUTRAGE TO GO UNPUNISHED.

CASTRATION SHOULD DO THE TRICK!
WHOA!

FIGHT, THIEF!
GO FOR YOUR SWORD INSTEAD OF TRAPPING MY MEN OUTSIDE!

AT LEAST DIE WITH A LITTLE HONOUR!

HONOUR BE DAMNED!!

WHY DIDN'T YOU TELL ME YOU WERE AN IMPERIAL SEDUCTRESS?
THE DANGER MAKES THE EXPERIENCE ALL THE MORE STIMULATING, WOULDN'T YOU AGREE?

SORRY TO LOVE YOU AND LEAVE YOU, LADY ZOYA.
THAT'S JUST LIFE...

MY LIFE!

THIS ISN'T MINE!

MANY THANKS, MILADY!
I'LL KEEP THIS! TREASURE IT FOREVER AS A MEMENTO OF OUR PASSION!

TSYGANOV BLACK MARKET, ST. PETERSBURG.
SEVEN HUNDRED AND FIFTY?!?
LOOK AT THOSE JEWELS. IT'S THE GENUINE ARTICLE—THE EROTICOSTUME OF AN IMPERIAL SEDUCTRESS!

NEXT PROG ▷ TSAR WARS!

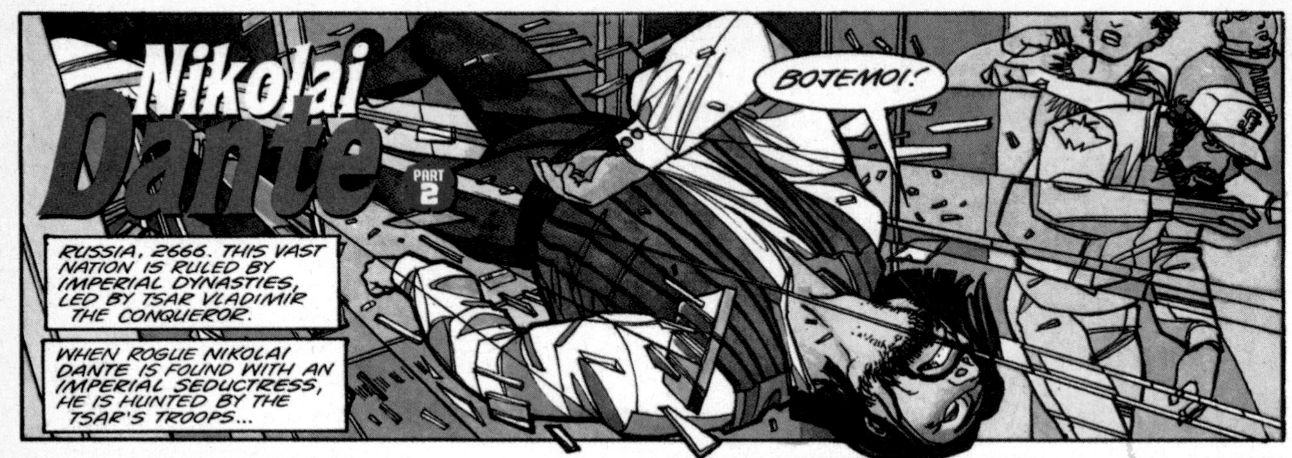
Nikolai Dante
PART 2
RUSSIA, 2666. THIS VAST NATION IS RULED BY IMPERIAL DYNASTIES, LED BY TSAR VLADIMIR THE CONQUEROR.
WHEN ROGUE NIKOLAI DANTE IS FOUND WITH AN IMPERIAL SEDUCTRESS, HE IS HUNTED BY THE TSAR'S TROOPS...
BOJEMOI!

THIS LOWBORN SWINE—THIS IS THE THIEF WHO DEFEATED CAPTAIN ARBATOV AND A SQUAD OF HUSSARS?

HARD TO BELIEVE, ISN'T IT?
DO YOU WISH ME TO BEAT HIM FURTHER, TSARINA?

TSARINA... YOU'RE JENA, THE TSAR'S DAUGHTER?
I'M SURPRISED A WOMAN OF YOUR POWER AND BEAUTY NEEDS SUCH CRUDE METHODS TO FIND YOURSELF A MAN.

I CONDUCT MY OWN BEATINGS, COMMANDER PYRE.

SCRIPT
ROBBIE MORRISON
ART
SIMON FRASER
LETTERS
ANNIE PARKHOUSE

THE IMPERIAL PALACE,
ST. PETERSBURG.

TAKE YOUR TIME WITH HIM, MONGOLIAN...
A LITTLE BLOODSPORT ALWAYS LIVENS UP DUNGEON LIFE.

YOU'LL NOT BE SO PRETTY, BOY, WHEN I DANCE ON YOUR FACE...

I'M NOT A DANCING MAN!

OUFFF!
GNNGF!

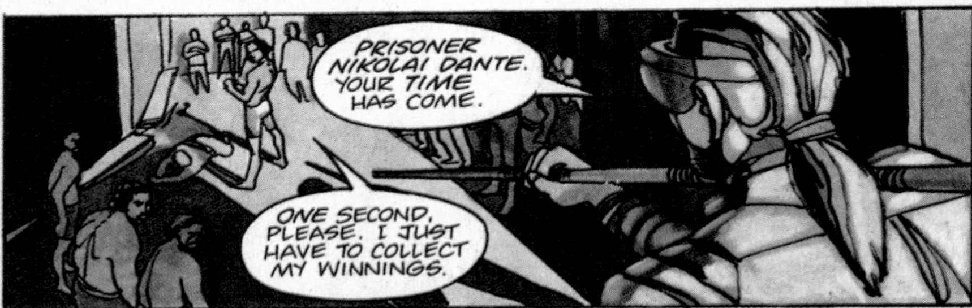
PRISONER NIKOLAI DANTE. YOUR TIME HAS COME.
ONE SECOND, PLEASE. I JUST HAVE TO COLLECT MY WINNINGS.

YOU WOULDN'T BE ADVERSE TO A LITTLE BRIBERY, WOULD YOU?
WHAT HAVE YOU GOT TO OFFER, THIEF?
TWO CIGAR-BUTTS, A THIMBLEFUL OF VODKA AND SOMETHING THAT SMELLS SUSPICIOUSLY LIKE CHEESE.

YOU FOUGHT THE MONGOLIAN FOR SUCH PETTY SPOILS!?
I'M A GAMBLING MAN. OLD HABITS DIE HARD.
BESIDES, THERE'S A LIMIT TO WHAT INMATES CAN CONCEAL IN THEIR PRISON PANTS.

WELL...
MOST INMATES...

THE COURT OF VLADIMIR THE CONQUEROR, TSAR OF ALL THE RUSSIAS, IS NOW IN SESSION.
PRISONERS! DO NOT WEEP OR BEG. UNDIGNIFIED SIGNS OF WEAKNESS OR REPENTANCE WILL RESULT ONLY IN HARSHER PUNISHMENT.
NIKOLAI DANTE! PREPARE TO FACE THE JUDGEMENT OF THE TSAR.

YOU MAY BEGIN, TSAR VLADIMIR.
I'M READY TO CONDUCT MY DEFENCE.
YOU *HAVE* NO DEFENCE, *BOY*.

NIKOLAI DANTE, SINCE ENTERING ST. PETERSBURG RELIABLE WITNESSES HAVE CONFIRMED YOUR *GUILT* IN THE FOLLOWING CRIMES—
BANDITRY, FRAUD, DECEIT, UNAUTHORISED *DUELLING* AND *SEDUCTION* FOR THE PURPOSES OF FINANCIAL GAIN.

THESE LAST CHARGES ARE... *INTERESTING*.
AN ASSAULT ON A *CAPTAIN ARBATOV*... AND A COMPLAINT FROM AN *IMPERIAL SEDUCTRESS*— YOU *STOLE* HER *UNDERWEAR*.

THEY WERE *A GIFT*, IN APPRECIATION OF *SERVICES RENDERED!*
I DON'T RESORT TO THIEVERY FOR ITEMS OF SUCH *INTIMATE APPAREL* —THEY'RE *HURLED* AT ME WITH *GREAT ABANDON*.

THESE CRIMES WERE *ALL* COMMITTED AGAINST RANKING MEMBERS OF THE IMPERIAL NOBILITY?
THERE'S NO *FUN* OR *PROFIT* IN THIEVING FROM THOSE WHO CAN'T AFFORD IT...

THAT'S THE WAY OF THE EMPIRE, *YOUNG DANTE*.
IF YOU CAN'T ACCEPT THAT, YOU DON'T DESERVE TO LIVE AS PART OF IT.

AND THAT *IS* THE PENALTY FOR OFFENCES AS GRAVE AS YOURS...
EXECUTION.
I'LL *HAPPILY* SUPERVISE, FATHER.

FOR A BRIGAND, HOWEVER, YOU'VE PROVEN YOURSELF ADMIRABLY RESOURCEFUL, AND NEW BLOOD IS ALWAYS HEALTHY FOR THE EMPIRE.
IN ADDITION TO A FULL PARDON, I OFFER YOU A COMMISSION IN THE RAVEN CORPS.
WHAT!?

I DEMAND HIS EXECUTION!
I WANT HIS HEAD!

JENA, MY LOVE.
DO NOT INTERFERE WITH MY WILL.

A COMMISSION IN THE RAVEN CORPS, EH...
AND WHAT— IF I MAY BE SO BOLD — IF I REFUSE?

I HAVE OTHER JUDGEMENTS TO MAKE THIS DAY, YOUNG DANTE.
OBSERVE THEM WHILE YOU DECIDE.
BRING FORWARD CAPTAIN ARBATOV AND HIS MEN.

HE FIGHTS WITHOUT HONOUR, TSAR VLADIMIR! HE'LL STAB YOU IN THE BACK THE FIRST CHANCE HE GETS!
HE'S A THIEF!

A THIEF WHO NONETHELESS DEFEATED A SQUAD OF HIGHLY TRAINED HUSSARS.
IMAGINE HOW THE MORALE OF MY OTHER TROOPS WOULD SUFFER IF I LET SUCH A FAILURE GO UNPUNISHED.
ARBATOV, YOU SOUGHT THE SERVICES OF A SEDUCTRESS WHILE COURTING MY DAUGHTER, JENA — AN INSULT TO IMPERIAL HONOUR!

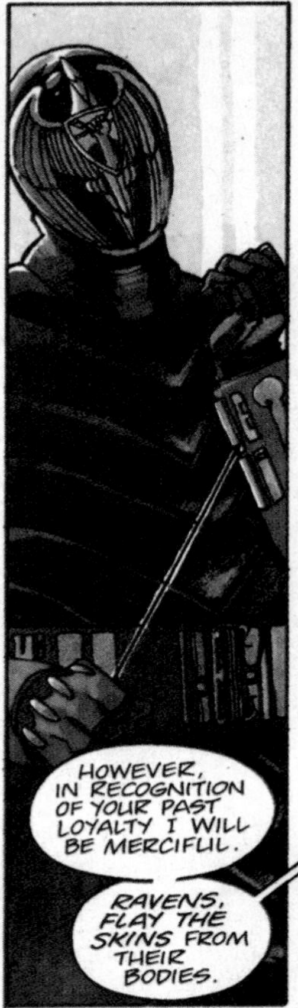

NEXT PROG ⮞ ALIENATION ZONE!

RUSSIA 2666.
THE IMPERIAL PALACE, ST. PETERSBURG.
Nikolai Dante
PART 3

WASH ME.
VIGOROUSLY.
SCRIPT ROBBIE MORRISON
ART SIMON FRASER
LETTERS ANNIE PARKHOUSE

AS YOU KNOW, TSAR VLADIMIR, ALL NEW ADMISSIONS TO THE PALACE DUNGEONS UNDERGO EXTENSIVE GENETIC SCANNING.

PRISONER NIKOLAI DANTE'S GENETIC HERITAGE AND BLOODLINE WERE UNMISTAKEABLE.
WHILE NOT A FULL-BLOODED MEMBER OF THE DYNASTY, THE PURITY OF HIS SYSTEM IS MORE THAN ENOUGH FOR YOUR PURPOSES.

I FEEL RATHER SORRY FOR HIM.
THE POOR BOY HAS ABSOLUTELY NO IDEA WHO OR WHAT HE IS.

HE'S AN ARROGANT THIEF...
I SPARED HIS LIFE BECAUSE OF YOUR DISCOVERY, PHYSICIAN.

IF YOU'RE MISTAKEN OR IF THE PLANS I HAVE FOR YOUNG DANTE FAIL...

...I WILL HAVE YOU ADMINISTERED WITH AN ENEMA.
A CORROSIVE ACID ENEMA.
ONE OF THE MOST EFFECTIVE TORTURES I DEVISED DURING THE PURGES, PYRE.
I WAS REMARKABLY IMAGINATIVE WHEN IT CAME TO DEALING WITH ENEMIES IN THE EARLY DAYS OF MY REIGN.
I THINK THE POWER WENT TO MY HEAD SLIGHTLY, MADE ME RATHER DECADENT.
DECADENT, TSAR VLADIMIR? YOU?
SURELY NOT.

MURMANSK.
THIS IS CAPTAIN DANTE OF THE IMPERIAL RAVEN CORPS.

STAND ASIDE OR FACE THE WRATH OF TSAR VLADIMIR THE CONQUEROR!

BOJEMOI!

SO MUCH FOR THE FEARSOME REPUTATION OF THE RAVEN CORPS!
ISN'T THE MERE SIGHT OF YOU MEANT TO HAVE THE PEASANTS FLEEING IN TERROR?
YOUR TACTICS WERE PATHETIC.
A TRUE RAVEN DOES NOT DEIGN TO SPEAK TO HIS ENEMIES.

AND A TRUE RAVEN NEVER SPARES THE LIVES OF THOSE WHO OPPOSE THE TSAR'S WILL.
YOU'VE A LOT TO LEARN, BOY.

I THINK I'VE LEARNED ENOUGH.

YOUR UNIFORM IS INCOMPLETE— YOU NEED A HEAD FOR YOUR BELT.
I'LL DONATE THIS ONE IF YOU LACK THE STOMACH TO CLAIM YOUR OWN.

OH, I'VE THE STOMACH ALRIGHT.
MAYBE I'LL TAKE YOURS.

THIS BICKERING ENDS NOW.
REMOUNT YOUR RAVENWINGS, THE OBJECTIVE OF OUR MISSION IS OVER THE NEXT HILL.

THE IMPERIAL FLEET ATTACKED AN UNIDENTIFIED STARSHIP AFTER IT ENTERED OUR ATMOSPHERE WITHOUT PERMISSION.
WE'RE TO INVESTIGATE THE WRECK AND REPORT OUR FINDINGS TO ST. PETERSBURG.

THERE SHE IS...

The environmental devastation of The Murmansk Alienation Zone began over five centuries ago, when a long-forgotten regime in its death throes abandoned its fleet of war machines to the Arctic ravages of the Barents Sea.
Over the decades, the graveyard of Murmansk grew inexorably to welcome the relics of the past and the lost ghosts that were said to haunt their decks.
RAVENS— CONCEAL YOURSELVES. SNIPER POSITIONING.
OUR NEW RECRUIT AND I WILL EXPLORE THE WRECK.

NEXT PROG ➲ BIRD OF PREY!

RUSSIA, 2666. ADVENTURER NIKOLAI DANTE HAS BEEN PRESSGANGED INTO JOINING THE TSAR'S RAVEN CORPS.

WHILE DANTE AND THE TSAR'S DAUGHTER, JENA, ARE INVESTIGATING A CRASHED STARSHIP IN THE MURMANSK ALIENATION ZONE, THEY ARE ATTACKED...

WHAT THE HELL IS THAT?!?

A ROMANOV BIRD OF PREY! IT'S PROGRAMMED TO PROTECT THEIR SHIP— IT WON'T STOP TILL WE'RE DEAD!

SSSKKREEEE

Nikolai Dante

Part 4

++ INTRUDERS RETREATING ++

++ ENGAGING PURSUIT MODE ++

DRAW ITS FIRE! I'LL CLIP ITS WINGS!

SCRIPT ROBBIE MORRISON

ART SIMON FRASER

LETTERS ANNIE PARKHOUSE

YOU, THIEF? IT'LL KILL YOU!

I'M TOO COOL TO KILL!

SSSKREEEEEE
BOJEMOI!
++ MINIMAL DAMAGE SUSTAINED ++

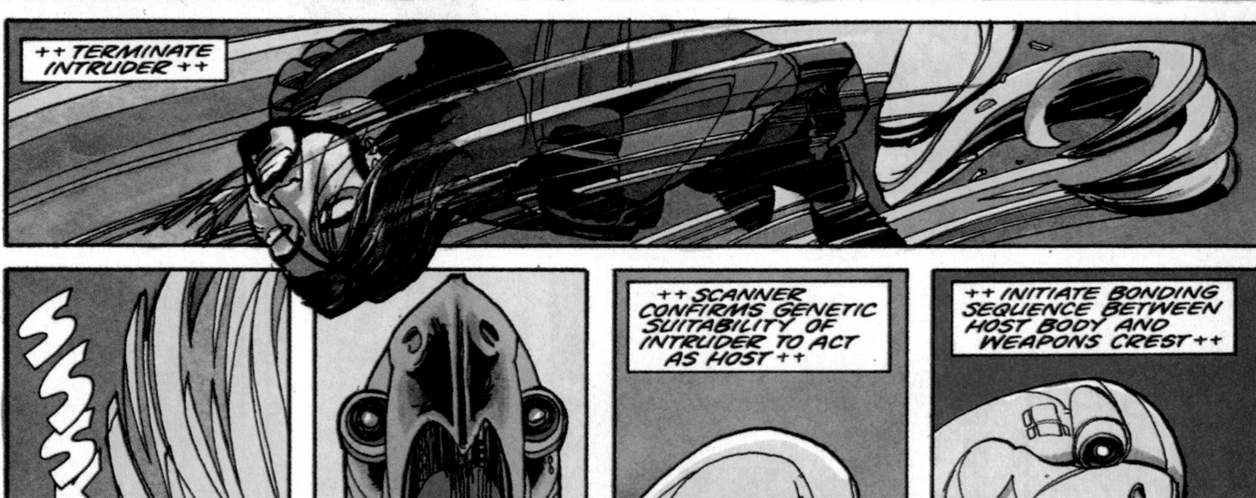
++ TERMINATE INTRUDER ++

SSSKKREEE

++ HALT TERMINATION ++

++ SCANNER CONFIRMS GENETIC SUITABILITY OF INTRUDER TO ACT AS HOST ++

++ INITIATE BONDING SEQUENCE BETWEEN HOST BODY AND WEAPONS CREST ++

AAAAGHKKK!
CONGRATULATIONS, NIKOLAI DANTE!
YOU'VE JUST BECOME THE MOST WANTED MAN IN THE EMPIRE.
AND I CAN'T THINK OF ANYONE MORE DESERVING OF THE HONOUR.
NOW, MOVE!
THE BIRD OF PREY HAS DEACTIVATED BECAUSE IT THINKS IT'S ACCOMPLISHED ITS MISSION — ITS MASTERS WON'T BE SO EASILY FOOLED.

WELL, WELL, IF IT ISN'T THE TSAR'S FAVOURITE DAUGHTER.
AN ILLUSTRIOUS VISITOR INDEED.
WHO?

PERMIT US TO INTRODUCE OURSELVES — FOR THE SAKE OF YOUR UNKEMPT COMPANION.
HONESTLY, JENA, I'D HAVE CREDITED YOU WITH BETTER TASTE IN MEN.

ALEKSANDR AND ALEKSANDRA ROMANOV.
HEIRS TO THE ROMANOV DYNASTY AND ALL ITS GLORIES. PAST, PRESENT AND FUTURE.

NOW THAT WE'VE DISPENSED WITH COURT FORMALITIES...
PLEASE EXPLAIN WHY YOU THOUGHT IT NECESSARY TO TRESPASS UPON OUR PROPERTY.

THE FORCES OF THE TSAR— YOUR RULER—MAY GO WHERE THEY PLEASE.
YOUR STARSHIP CRASHED. WE, UH, WERE IN THE VICINITY AND INITIATED A SEARCH FOR SURVIVORS.

HOW VERY BENEVOLENT OF YOU—CONSIDERING IT WAS MORE THAN LIKELY THE TSARIST FLEET THAT BROUGHT HER DOWN IN THE FIRST PLACE.
YET ANOTHER DESPERATE ATTEMPT TO GAIN POSSESSION OF THE ROMANOV POWER SOURCE.

I DON'T CARE FOR YOUR ACCUSATIONS, ROMANOV!

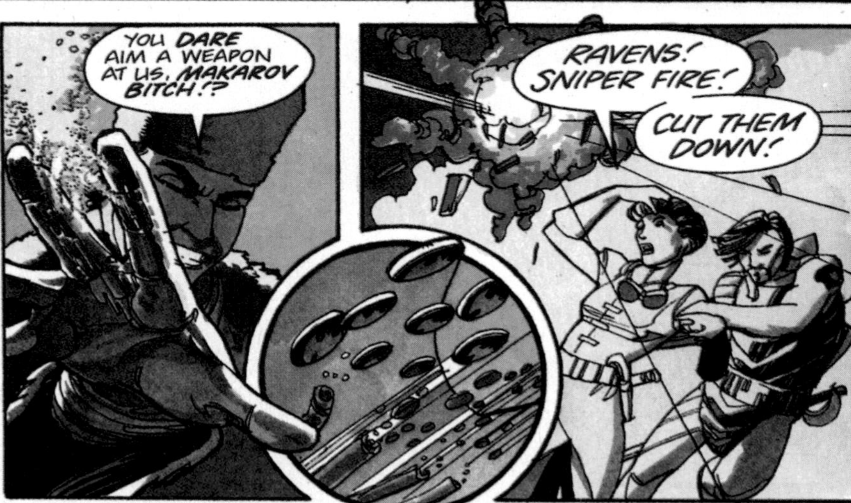
YOU DARE AIM A WEAPON AT US, MAKAROV BITCH!?
RAVENS! SNIPER FIRE!
CUT THEM DOWN!

BRRRAK

AHHHH!

BOJEMOI!

NEXT PROG ⏩ DOUBLE TROUBLE!

IN THE MURMANSK ALIENATION ZONE NIKOLAI DANTE HAS BEEN BONDED TO A HOUSE OF ROMANOV BIO-CREST, MAKING HIM THE MOST WANTED MAN IN THE EMPIRE.
NOW HE IS IN THE MIDDLE OF A PITCHED BATTLE BETWEEN THE RAVEN CORPS, LED BY THE TSAR'S DAUGHTER JENA, AND ROMANOV TWINS ALEKSANDR AND ALEKSANDRA...
Nikolai Dante
PART 5

IT MUST BE TRUE WHAT THEY SAY IN THE RAVEN CORPS...

THERE'S NO GREATER HONOUR THAN TO LAY DOWN YOUR LIFE FOR THE TSAR.
THEY CERTAINLY SEEM MORE THAN WILLING TO DIE TODAY...
SCRIPT ROBBIE MORRISON
ART SIMON FRASER
LETTERS ANNIE PARKHOUSE

DANTE! YOU'RE AN OFFICER IN THE RAVEN CORPS! AID YOUR COMRADES!
JENA, MY COMRADES WOULD GLADLY DANGLE ME FROM THE GALLOWS IF THEY HAD THE CHANCE...

ANYWAY, THIS DAMNED EAGLE'S KILLING ME ALREADY.
I HAVEN'T FELT THIS BAD SINCE CHALLENGING PAPA YELTSIN TO A VODKA-SWILLING CONTEST...

BOJEMOI! WHAT'S HAPPENING TO MY HANDS?!?

THERE'S A RAVEN CLAWING AT YOUR BACK, BROTHER.
REALLY?

I HADN'T NOTICED— I ONLY HAVE EYES FOR YOU.
YOU DEVIL, YOU ALWAYS SAY THE RIGHT THINGS.

HHAAAAGGKKK!!
AND YOU STEAL THE HEART OF EVERY MAN YOU MEET, YOU SHAMELESS HUSSY...

MMMMNN!
OOOOOHHH!

YOU SHOULD BE IN THE BOLSHOI, ALEKSANDRA.

YOU DANCE DIVINELY!
WHY, SIR, HOW COULD I POSSIBLY DO OTHERWISE WITH SUCH A GALLANT GENTLEMAN FOR A PARTNER?

NOW, JENA, HOW SHOULD WE HANDLE YOUR INDISCRETION?
REVEAL IT TO THE EMPIRE AND CAUSE A MAJOR DYNASTIC SCANDAL?

OR PUNISH IT NOW WITH A QUIET EXECUTION?
BOTH OPTIONS ARE VERY TEMPTING.

YOU'D DO WELL TO FOLLOW YOUR COMPANION'S LEAD— PROSTRATE YOURSELF BEFORE US WHILE WE DECIDE.
IT'S PATHETIC, BUT ALSO GRATIFYING, TO SEE A MAN BEG IN SUCH A WAY.
IT MAKES YOU REALISE HOW SUPERIOR WE ROMANOVS ARE TO THE REST OF THE EMPIRE.

THERE'S BLOOD ON MY BOOT. LICK IT OFF, AND PERHAPS I'LL SPARE YOU.

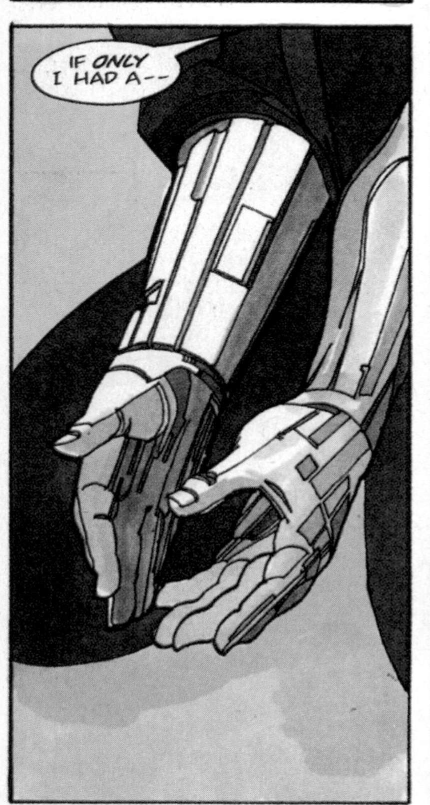
IF ONLY I HAD A--

A WEAPON?!?

COME ON, BE QUICK ABOUT IT.

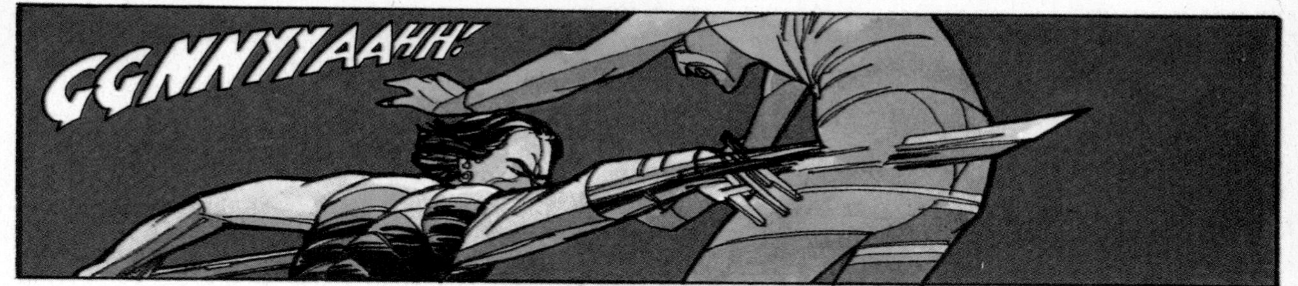
GGNNYYAAHH!

I'M NOT A BEGGING MAN!

ALEKSANDRA! HE BEARS THE CREST!
IMPOSSIBLE! ONLY A ROMANOV BORN MAY BEAR A WEAPONS CREST!

AAAACHKK!

COME ON, JENA!

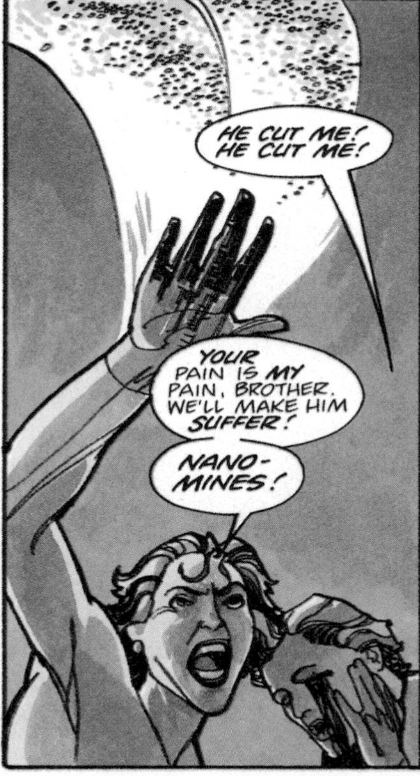
HE CUT ME! HE CUT ME!
YOUR PAIN IS MY PAIN, BROTHER. WE'LL MAKE HIM SUFFER!
NANO-MINES!

YOU KNOW HOW TO SHOW A MAN A GOOD TIME, JENA. I'VE BOOZED MY WAY ACROSS HALF THE EMPIRE AND NEVER EVEN WOKEN UP WITH A TATTOO...
ONE DAY IN YOUR COMPANY AND I GET A GARGOYLE GRAFTED TO MY SHOULDER!

NOT TO MENTION THESE BEAUTIES.
WHAT THE HELL'S GOING ON?
YOU'RE AN OFFICER OF THE RAVEN CORPS. INFORMATION IS RELAYED TO YOU ONLY ON A NEED-TO-KNOW BASIS.

IS THAT A FACT? PERHAPS OUR TWIN ADMIRERS WILL BE MORE OBLIGING...
THIS WAS MEANT TO BE A SIMPLE EXTRACTION, ALEKSANDR. WE SHOULD CALL FOR BACK-UP.

THIS IS A MATTER OF HONOUR, ALEKSANDRA. HE CUT ME!
WE'LL HUNT HIM ALONE, THEN DRAG HIS CARCASS BACK TO THE WINTER PALACE FOR EXAMINATION.

YOU'RE A RECKLESS ONE, THIEF.
WHY, TSARINA JENA—FLATTERY'LL GET YOU EVERYWHERE...

THE ROMANOV DYNASTY HAVE DEVELOPED THE MOST POWERFUL BIO-WEAPON IN THE EMPIRE, FASHIONED IN THE FORM OF THEIR ANCIENT COAT-OF-ARMS.
THE WEAPONS CREST POSES A GREAT THREAT TO THE TSAR'S REIGN. HE MUST LEARN ITS SECRETS AND DEVELOP SIMILAR TECHNOLOGY FOR HIS OWN FORCES.

'THE WEAPONS CREST SYMBIOTICALLY **BONDS** ONLY WITH THE **ROMANOV ELITE**. THEIR GENETIC PURITY HAS BEEN ENHANCED BY A BREEDING PROGRAMME INITIATED BY **DIMITRI ROMANOV, DYNASTY PATRIARCH**, TO STRENGTHEN THEIR FALSE CLAIM TO THE EMPIRE.

'**BEARING THE CREST** GIVES THE ROMANOVS COMBAT CAPABILITIES UNIQUELY ATTUNED TO THEIR INDIVIDUAL PHYSICAL AND PSYCHOLOGICAL PROFILES.

'IT MANIFESTS ITSELF AS **NANOTECHNOLOGY** IN THE TWINS, FILLING THEIR SYSTEMS WITH **MICROSCOPIC DROIDS** WHICH CAN HEAL ALMOST ANY WOUND, FORM **BIO-BLADES** OR BE LAUNCHED FROM THE BODY AS INVISIBLE EXPLOSIVES.

'THE CRESTS ARE PRODUCED BY UNKNOWN TECHNOLOGY AT A SECRET OFFWORLD LOCATION. WE INTERCEPTED THE TRANSPORTATION OF THE LATEST ONE — **WITH YOU**!'

NEXT PROG ⏩ SIBLING RIVALRY!

IN THE MURMANSK ALIENATION ZONE NIKOLAI DANTE HAS BEEN BONDED WITH A ROMANOV BIO-CREST, MAKING HIM THE MOST WANTED MAN IN THE EMPIRE.
NOW DANTE HAS LEARNED FROM THE TSAR'S DAUGHTER JENA THAT HE IS OF ARISTOCRATIC BLOOD...

A GENESCAN CONFIRMED YOUR HERITAGE WHILE YOU WERE IN IMPERIAL CUSTODY. NO DOUBT ABOUT IT, YOU'RE A ROMANOV, ALRIGHT.
BASTARD SON OF A NOBLE HOUSE, EH ...
Nikolai Dante
SCRIPT ROBBIE MORRISON
ART SIMON FRASER
COLOURS ALISON KIRKPATRICK
LETTERS ANNIE PARKHOUSE
PART 6

YOU DIDN'T KNOW YOUR PARENTS?
ONLY MAMA — KATARINA DANTE.
SHE WASN'T VERY SPECIFIC ABOUT MY FATHER'S IDENTITY...

KATARINA DANTE!? THE PIRATE-QUEEN!?
SHE ABANDONED ME WHEN I WAS 11 OR 12, I'M NOT SURE WHICH...

SHE INSISTS ON ROBBING THE EMPIRE BLIND WITH AN ALL-FEMALE CREW.
THEY DIDN'T HAVE MUCH IN THE WAY OF MALE FACILITIES, AND I WAS AN EARLY DEVELOPER.

WELL, JENA, YOU'VE GOT YOUR PRECIOUS WEAPONS CREST — AND ME INTO THE BARGAIN. NOW WHAT?
WE EVADE THE ROMANOVS AND RETURN TO ST. PETERSBURG.

WHERE I'LL BE SLICED AND DICED BY THE TSAR'S SCIENTISTS AS THEY TRY TO UNLOCK THE SECRETS OF THE CREST AND ADAPT IT FOR IMPERIAL USE.
YOU'LL BE HANDSOMELY REWARDED, THIEF.
IF YOU SURVIVE.

USURPER OF THE ROMANOV CREST!
OUR CRESTS CAN TRACK YOURS WITHOUT FAIL!
YOU CANNOT ESCAPE!

THE HULL OF YOUR CRAFT IS BREACHED IN SEVERAL PLACES! IT CANNOT REMAIN AFLOAT FOR LONG!
YOU HAVE THREE CHOICES! SURRENDER AND WE MAY BE MERCIFUL! FACE US IN COMBAT AND DIE!

OR DROWN AND WE'LL TRAWL FOR YOUR CORPSE LATER!
DECIDE!

YOU WANT ME, YOU NOBLE SCUM!? COME AND GET ME!
JENA, MAKE YOUR WAY DOWN THE CORRIDOR, USE ONE OF THEIR BREACHES TO ESCAPE. I'LL KEEP THEM BUSY.
WHAT!?

YOU HEARD THEM, I CAN'T ESCAPE — BUT YOU CAN. YOU'RE THE FUTURE EMPRESS OF OUR WORLD. YOU HAVE TO LIVE!

I'M JUST A THIEF. LIVE OR DIE, I'M NOTHING.
BUT IN THE BRIEF TIME WE'VE HAD TOGETHER, JENA MAKAROV, I'VE KNOWN HONOUR AND NOBILITY... MAYBE EVEN LOVE.

NIKOLAI...

THINK OF ME, MILADY?
SOMETIMES?

THE THINGS I SAY TO GET INTO PEOPLE'S PANTS!

WHOA! HOLD YOUR FIRE! I'M WITH YOU!
I'M ONE OF YOU!

OUR PREY'S CHANGED HIS TUNE. NOBLE SCUM? WASN'T THAT WHAT HE CALLED US?
I SAID THAT TO SEND THE TSARINA ON HER WAY.
PRECIPITATING A CONFLICT WITH THE TSAR IS THE LAST THING WE ROMANOVS NEED. NO?

WE ROMANOVS?
OF COURSE!
I'VE NO IDEA WHO DID THE DIRTY DEED, BUT MY FATHER IS A ROMANOV. HOW ELSE COULD THE CREST HAVE BONDED WITH ME?

I'M READY TO TAKE MY RIGHTFUL PLACE IN THE ROMANOV DYNASTY AND ACCEPT THE RESPONSIBILITIES OF MY HERITAGE...
AND, I SUPPOSE, WHATEVER WEALTH THAT ENTAILS...

DID YOU HEAR THAT ALEKSANDR? A NEW ADDITION TO THE FAMILY!
WHAT THRILLING TIMES WE COULD HAVE TOGETHER! WHAT FUN...

IF HE WASN'T A SEWER-BRED BASTARD!!
WOOAARRGH!

PRECEDENCE IS EVERYTHING TO AN IMPERIAL DYNASTY.
WE ROMANOVS HAVE STRIVED AFTER GENETIC PURITY FOR GENERATIONS...
YOU THINK WE'D LET A HALF-BLOOD LIKE YOU JOIN US!?

I DON'T THINK WE SHOULD EVEN TAINT OUR BIO-BLADES WITH YOUR BASTARD BLOOD...
JUST IN CASE WE CATCH SOMETHING...

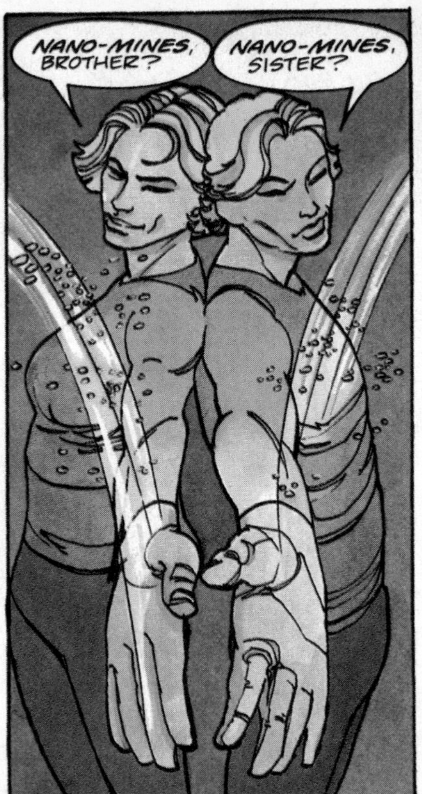
NANO-MINES, BROTHER?
NANO-MINES, SISTER?

TELL ME, I'VE BEEN AN ONLY CHILD FOR 20-ODD YEARS...
IS THIS WHAT THEY MEAN BY SIBLING RIVALRY?

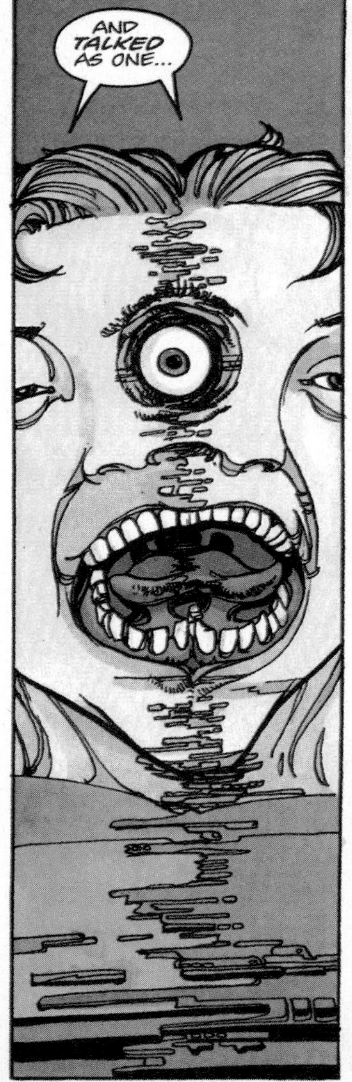

BUT OUR MOST CHERISHED DREAM ONLY BECAME REALITY WHEN FATHER BLESSED US WITH OUR WEAPONS CRESTS...

AND ALLOWED US TO BECOME ONE!

BOJEMOI!

IN THE MURMANSK ALIENATION ZONE **NIKOLAI DANTE** HAS BEEN BONDED WITH A ROMANOV **BIO-CREST**, MAKING HIM THE MOST WANTED MAN IN THE EMPIRE.

NOW DANTE FIGHTS ROMANOV TWINS ALEKSANDR AND ALEKSANDRA, WHO HAVE **MERGED** WITH EACH OTHER...

IMPRESSIVE SIGHT, AREN'T WE? BOTH MALE **AND** FEMALE.

THE **PERFECT BEING**!

Nikolai Dante

PART 7

WHICH PART OF THE PERFECT BEING DID THAT HURT MOST?

MALE OR FEMALE?

YOU'LL NEVER BE A TRUE ROMANOV!

BOJEMOI!!

A LOWBORN BASTARD— THAT'S ALL YOU ARE, ALL YOU'LL EVER BE!

AT LEAST DO THE ROMANOV BLOODLINE THE COURTESY OF DYING WITH HONOUR!
HONOUR BE DAMNED!!
AARRGGHHHHHH!!

HHEELLPP MMEEEEEEEE

IF I'D HAD THE ARISTOCRATIC UPBRINGING YOU THINK ME SO UNWORTHY OF, I MIGHT ENGAGE IN ACTS OF SELFLESS NOBILITY...
...BUT I DOUBT IT!
YOU HAVE PROVED YOURSELF WORTHY. YOU ARE ONE OF US
YOU ARE A ROMANOV!
THE NAME'S DANTE. NIKOLAI DANTE.
THE WORLD IS GOING TO BE HEARING A LOT OF IT.
IT'S THE LAST THING YOU'LL EVER HEAR!

YOU HAVE A DISTINCT TALENT FOR SURVIVAL, NIKOLAI DANTE.

LIKE I SAID, JENA...
I'M JUST TOO COOL TO KILL.

I'M BEGINNING TO THINK YOUR NOBLE SACRIFICE OF EARLIER WAS SOMEWHAT LESS-THAN-SINCERE.
WOMEN ARE ALWAYS SUSPICIOUS OF ME...

WITH GOOD REASON.
YOUR COMMISSION IN THE RAVEN CORPS IS HEREBY REVOKED. CONSIDER YOURSELF MY PRISONER.
I LIKE BEING MY OWN MAN. YOU WANT MY FREEDOM, YOU'LL HAVE TO TAME ME FIRST.
THINK YOU'RE WOMAN ENOUGH?

I WAS TRAINED IN THE ARTS OF WAR BY THE FINEST MILITARY COMMANDERS IN THE EMPIRE.

AND I LEARNED TO FIGHT IN THE SLEAZIEST BARS OF THE THIEVES' WORLD.
LET'S GET IT ON!

EN GARDE, THIEF!

Y'KNOW, JENA?
THERE ARE BETTER WAYS TO TAME A MAN...

WHY DON'T WE SLIP OUT OF THESE WET CLOTHES AND I'LL SHOW YOU A FEW?

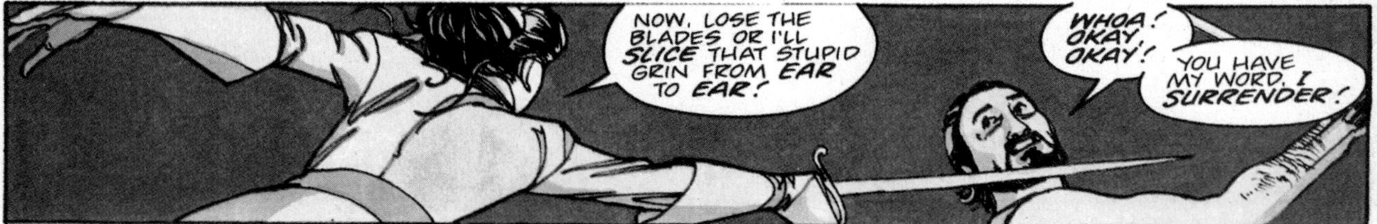

NEXT PROG ⏩ THE ROMANOV DYNASTY!

THE ROMANOV DYNASTY

Script: Robbie Morrison

Art: Simon Fraser

Colors: Alison Kirkpatrick

Letters: Ellie de Ville, Annie Parkhouse

Originally published in *2000 AD* Progs 1042-1049

In The Year Of The Tsar 2666, young men of good breeding should, while pursuing their goals and ambitions with dedication and determination...
...always ensure that their manners are decorous and praiseworthy.
—'ETIQUETTE OF AN IMPERIAL GENTLEMAN' —UPDATED EDITION.
Nikolai Dante
THE ROMANOV DYNASTY PART 1
SCRIPT ROBBIE MORRISON
ART SIMON FRASER
COLOURS ALISON KIRKPATRICK
LETTERS ELLIE DE VILLE
THE WINTER PALACE OF THE ROMANOV DYNASTY.
SO!
WHICH ONE OF YOU NOBLE SCUMBAGS IS MY FATHER!?

FOR YOUR SAKE, BOY...

I HOPE THERE'S MORE TO YOUR CLAIM THAN SIMPLE INSANITY OR DELUSIONS OF GRANDEUR.

THE NAME'S DANTE. NIKOLAI DANTE.
AND THERE'S A LOT MORE TO ME THAN MEETS THE EYE— ONLY A ROMANOV BORN CAN BEAR THE CREST!

AND WHAT DO YOU EXPECT TO CLAIM AS YOUR BIRTHRIGHT?
NOTHING TOO OSTENTATIOUS, LORD DMITRI.
POWER, RANK, WEALTH, USE OF THE ROMANOV HAREM, OR A PRIVATE ONE OF MY OWN.

MAYBE A TITLE— COUNT DANTE'S GOT A CERTAIN RING TO IT.

BEARING THE CREST AND BEING WORTHY OF IT ARE ENTIRELY DIFFERENT THINGS, BOY.

I DISPATCHED TWO OF MY FAMILY TO RECOVER THAT CREST. SHOULD I ASSUME YOU HAVE SINCE DISPATCHED THEM FROM THIS WORLD?
I ESCAPED THE TSAR'S FORCES IMMEDIATELY AFTER THEY FORCED ME TO BOND WITH THE CREST. I ENCOUNTERED NO ROMANOVS UNTIL ARRIVING HERE.

AND IT TEARS AT MY HEART TO THINK THAT I MAY HAVE LOST BROTHERS OR SISTERS WITHOUT EVER MEETING THEM...

ALMOST AS MUCH AS IT TURNS MY STOMACH TO HEAR YOUR LIES, THIEF!

JENA MAKAROV, THE TSAR'S DAUGHTER. WE CAUGHT HER SCALING THE NORTH FACE. SENT THREE MEN TO THEIR DEATHS BEFORE WE OVERPOWERED HER.
THIS MAN, NIKOLAI DANTE, IS A FUGITIVE FROM IMPERIAL JUSTICE!

THE TREACHEROUS SWINE DECEIVED ME IN MURMANSK– I'VE PURSUED HIM OVER HALF THE EMPIRE.
HAND HIM OVER IN THE NAME OF THE TSAR!

DON'T ADDRESS US AS IF WE WERE YOUR SUBJECTS, GIRL.
THE ROMANOV DYNASTY HAS A FAR GREATER CLAIM TO THE THRONE THAN YOUR OWN.

YOU SHOULDN'T BE SO ARROGANT, LORD DMITRI. NOT WHEN TWO OF YOUR CHILDREN ARE MISSING.
PERHAPS YOUR WEAPONS CRESTS AREN'T AS INVINCIBLE AS YOU THINK.

Are you trying to get us both killed!?
The only thing I'm devoting my life to seeing killed is you, Dante!

DON'T LISTEN TO HER, LORD DMITRI!
SHE SUFFERS FROM WINDSOR SYNDROME. POWER AND WEALTH HAVE DRIVEN HER MAD– SHE CHASES ME AROUND LIKE A LUST-CRAZED SEDUCTRESS.

WHERE ARE ALEKSANDR AND ALEKSANDRA?
AT THE BOTTOM OF THE BARENTS SEA.
THEY LAUNCHED AN UNPROVOKED ATTACK ON THE RAVEN CORPS, AND PAID THE PRICE ALL THE TSAR'S ENEMIES PAY.

I WOULDN'T BE A GOOD FATHER IF I DIDN'T SEEK RETRIBUTION.
LET THE RECORDS SHOW THAT JENA MAKAROV RECEIVED THE FAIREST OF TRIALS.

PROVE YOUR LOYALTY TO US, YOUNG DANTE!
EXECUTE THE MAKAROV BITCH. SLOWLY AND PAINFULLY.

Jena...

FATHER!
SOMETHING'S APPROACHING THE WINTER PALACE—FAR BIGGER THAN ANY KNOWN IMPERIAL BATTLECRAFT!
OPEN THE OBSERVATION BAY.

BOJEMOI!
DID YOU REALLY THINK I'D ENTER THIS EAGLES' NEST WITHOUT A FEW MINOR PRECAUTIONS?
THE IMPERIAL PALACE!

NEXT PROG ⏩ 'COME AND HAVE A GO IF YOU THINK YOU'RE HARD ENOUGH...'

Nikolai Dante

SCRIPT ROBBIE MORRISON
ART SIMON FRASER
COLOURS ALISON KIRKPATRICK
LETTERS ELLIE DE VILLE

THE ROMANOV DYNASTY PART 2

NIKOLAI DANTE HAS COME TO THE ROMANOV DYNASTY'S WINTER PALACE TO CLAIM HIS BIRTHRIGHT, USING THE BIO-CREST AS PROOF OF HIS NOBLE HERITAGE.

THE TSAR OF ALL RUSSIAS HAS COME IN HIS FLYING IMPERIAL PALACE TO CLAIM DANTE, THREATING WAR IF THE ROMANOVS DO NOT HAND HIM OVER...

BLOOD IS INDEED THICKER THAN WATER, BUT IT SATISFIES THE THIRST MORE.
I LOOK FORWARD TO SAMPLING YOURS, BOY.

THERE'S LITTLE POINT IN CONTINUING THIS DISCUSSION AT THE MOMENT. WE WILL RECONVENE WITH OUR COUNCILS OF WAR IN ATTENDANCE. THREE HOURS?
AGREED.

BEFORE WE PART, THERE IS A SMALL MATTER OF PERSONAL HONOUR TO BE SETTLED.
CAPTAIN?
DANTE, YOU THIEVING DOG!
I AM CAPTAIN ARBATOV OF THE TSAR'S OWN CUIRASSEIRS!

MY BROTHER WAS SKINNED ALIVE BECAUSE OF YOU!

I DEMAND SATISFACTION THROUGH TRIAL BY COMBAT!

HE WAS CHALLENGING YOU TO A DUEL.
WELL, HE LOST.
A FORMAL DUEL. ARRANGED TIMES, CHOICE OF WEAPONS.

THE ROMANOVS ARE THE OLDEST IMPERIAL DYNASTY, STRONG UPHOLDERS OF FORMALITY AND TRADITION.
YOU'RE MEANT TO BECOME PART OF THAT?

GIVE YOU ENOUGH ROPE, THIEF, YOU'RE SURE TO HANG YOURSELF.

DANTE'S IMPUDENCE CANNOT GO UNPUNISHED— WE'LL FIND SOME OTHER WAY OF DEFUSING THE ROMANOV CREST.
WHO AMONGST THE SCARLET WRAITHS IS BEST QUALIFIED TO ASSASSINATE HIM?
I AM, TSAR VLADIMIR.

IF APPREHENDED, THE ASSASSIN MUST BE SEEN TO BE ACTING ON THEIR OWN.
YOU'RE MY LORD PROTECTOR, PYRE. I CAN'T RISK LOSING YOU.
THEN MARALIS.
UUHHH...

YOUR CONSORT?
SHE'S AS LOYAL TO YOU AS I AM, SIRE.
YOUR HONOUR AND DEDICATION TO DUTY ARE ADMIRABLE, PYRE...

AS WAS THAT OF THE ARBATOVS. THEIR FAMILY WAS ONCE A MOST EFFICIENT PART OF THE MILITARY MACHINE.
HOW THE MIGHTY HAVE FALLEN...

THE ROMANOV WEAPONS RESEARCH FACILITY.
BEARING THE WEAPONS CREST AND THE CYBORGANIC TECHNOLOGY WITHIN IT GIVES THE ROMANOV ELITE COMBAT CAPABILITIES UNIQUELY ATTUNED TO THEIR INDIVIDUAL CHARACTERS.
BUT YOU'RE A HALF-BREED, LITTLE BROTHER. DON'T EXPECT TOO MUCH.
PERHAPS IT'S DUE TO YOUR SHALLOW NATURE, BUT YOUR CREST MANIFESTS ITSELF AS LITTLE MORE THAN BIO-BLADES, HEIGHTENED SENSES, A MINOR PHYSICAL HEALING FACTOR AND A SYMBIOTIC BATTLE COMPUTER THAT RESPONDS ONLY TO YOU.
IT HASN'T BEEN VERY RESPONSIVE SO FAR...
Your words carry such little substance that they deserve no response.
DIAVOLO!
IT'S IN MY HEAD!
Please maintain a semblance of dignity.
In addition to combat duties, I am bound to educate you in the ways of the aristocracy and mould you into a potential ruler of the Empire.
Not an easy task.

CAN'T YOU JUST ACCESS DYNASTY RECORDS TO FIND OUT WHICH OF THE RANDY ROMANOVS SIRED ME?
There are strange gaps in my databanks — no doubt due to having bonded with your inferior genes.

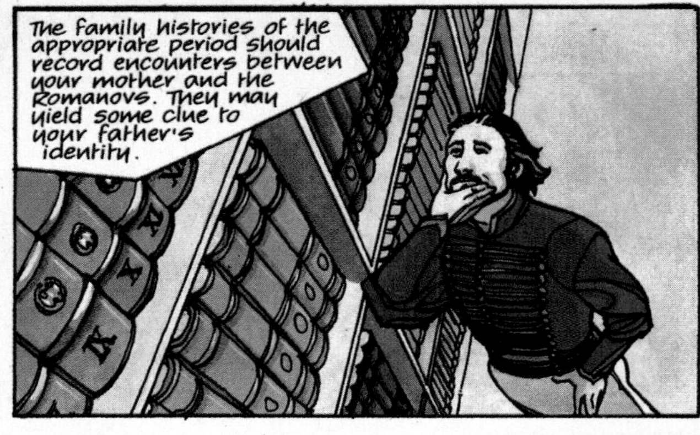
The family histories of the appropriate period should record encounters between your mother and the Romanovs. They may yield some clue to your father's identity.

Don't move your lips when you read. People will think you've an uneducated barbarian.
I AM.
AND PROUD OF IT.

FROM WHAT I WAS TOLD, I SAW YOU MORE AS A MAN OF ACTION THAN A MAN OF WORDS, NIKOLAI DANTE.
APPEARANCES CAN BE DECEIVING.
YOU DON'T LOOK LIKE ANY LIBRARIAN I'VE EVER SEEN BEFORE.

LIBRARIAN?
THE TSAR'S IS NOT THE ONLY DYNASTY THAT EMPLOYS SEDUCTRESSES. WE'VE BEEN TOLD TO EXTEND EVERY POSSIBLE HOSPITALITY TO YOU.

Dante. Things are not as they seem...
ADVISE ME ALL YOU WANT IN OTHER MATTERS, CREST, BUT IF THERE'S ONE THING I KNOW, IT'S WOMEN.

THE VOICE OF EXPERIENCE...
THERE'S AN OLD SAYING — 'COME AND HAVE A GO IF YOU THINK YOU'RE HARD ENOUGH.'

You are currently locked in a rather less-than-erotic embrace with an Abraxian Shapeshifter in the service of the Tsar.

It is, however, the female of the species...

BOJEMOI!

NEXT PROG ▷ THE ART OF DIPLOMACY!

NIKOLAI DANTE IS NOW A MEMBER OF THE ROMANOV DYNASTY, THANKS TO THE SENTIENT WEAPONS BIO-CREST BONDED TO HIS BODY.

BUT DANTE'S PRESENCE AT THE ROMANOV WINTER PALACE THREATENS TO CAUSE WAR WITH THE TSAR, WHO'S FLYING IMPERIAL PALACE IS NEARBY.

DANTE'S SEARCH TO FIND WHICH ROMANOV IS HIS FATHER TOOK HIM TO THE DYNASTY'S LIBRARY, WHERE A BEAUTIFUL WOMAN CATCHES HIS EYE.

Nikolai Dante
UNFORTUNATELY, SHE IS ACTUALLY A SHAPE-SHIFTING ALIEN SENT BY THE TSAR TO ASSASSINATE DANTE.
THE ROMANOV DYNASTY PART 3
SCRIPT ROBBIE MORRISON
ART SIMON FRASER
COLOURS ALISON KIRKPATRICK
LETTERS ANNIE PARKHOUSE

HHHLLGH!

YOU SHOULD BE WARY OF WHO AND WHAT YOU KISS, THIEF!

AAAAKK!

CREST?
HOW COME EVERY WOMAN WHO HITS ON ME THESE DAYS TURNS OUT TO BE AN ALIEN SHAPESHIFTER AFTER MY BLOOD INSTEAD OF MY OTHER BODILY FLUIDS?
Perhaps you've overestimated your appeal to the opposite sex.

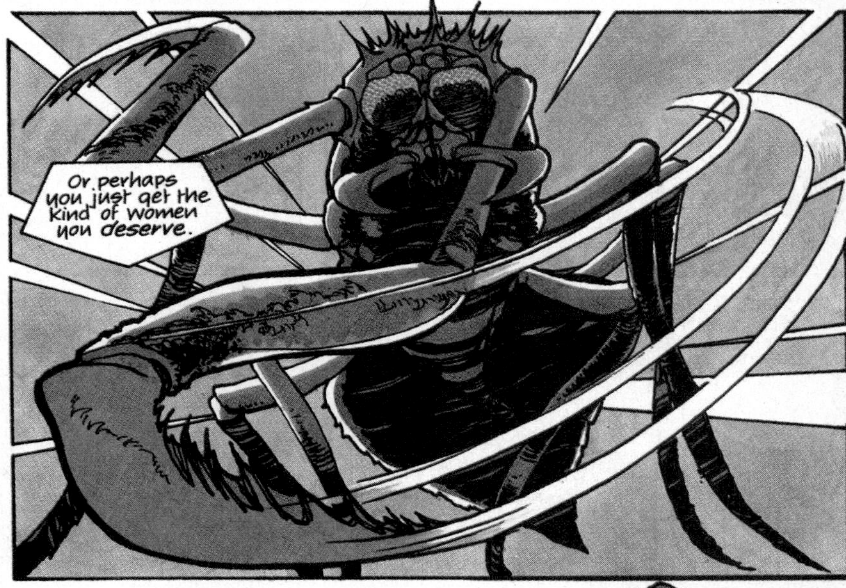
Or perhaps you just get the kind of women you deserve.

Y'KNOW, CREST, SOMETHING TELLS ME THIS ISN'T THE BEGINNING OF A BEAUTIFUL FRIENDSHIP.

HHAAAAIII!
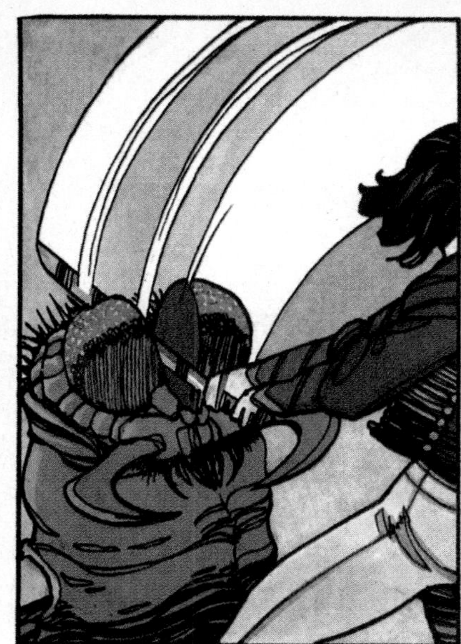

HUH?

HMPH!

SURRENDER, THIEF!

YOU HAVEN'T A CHANCE.

THE GREATEST PREDATORS IN ALL THE EMPIRE ARE MINE TO BECOME!!

THE IMPERIAL PALACE AND THE WINTER PALACE.
THIS IS BECOMING FARCICAL, DMITRI...
THAT TWO GREAT HOUSES SUCH AS OURS CAN BE TREATED SO IGNOBLY. HERE WE ARE ON THE BRINK OF WAR—
A WAR OF YOUR INSTIGATION, VLADIMIR.
—AND THE MAIN OBJECT OF OUR DISPUTE HASN'T EVEN DEIGNED TO SHOW HIS FACE.
WHERE IS NIKOLAI DANTE?

NOT TOO LATE TO DROP IN, IS IT?

NEXT PROG ⏩ DEVILS!

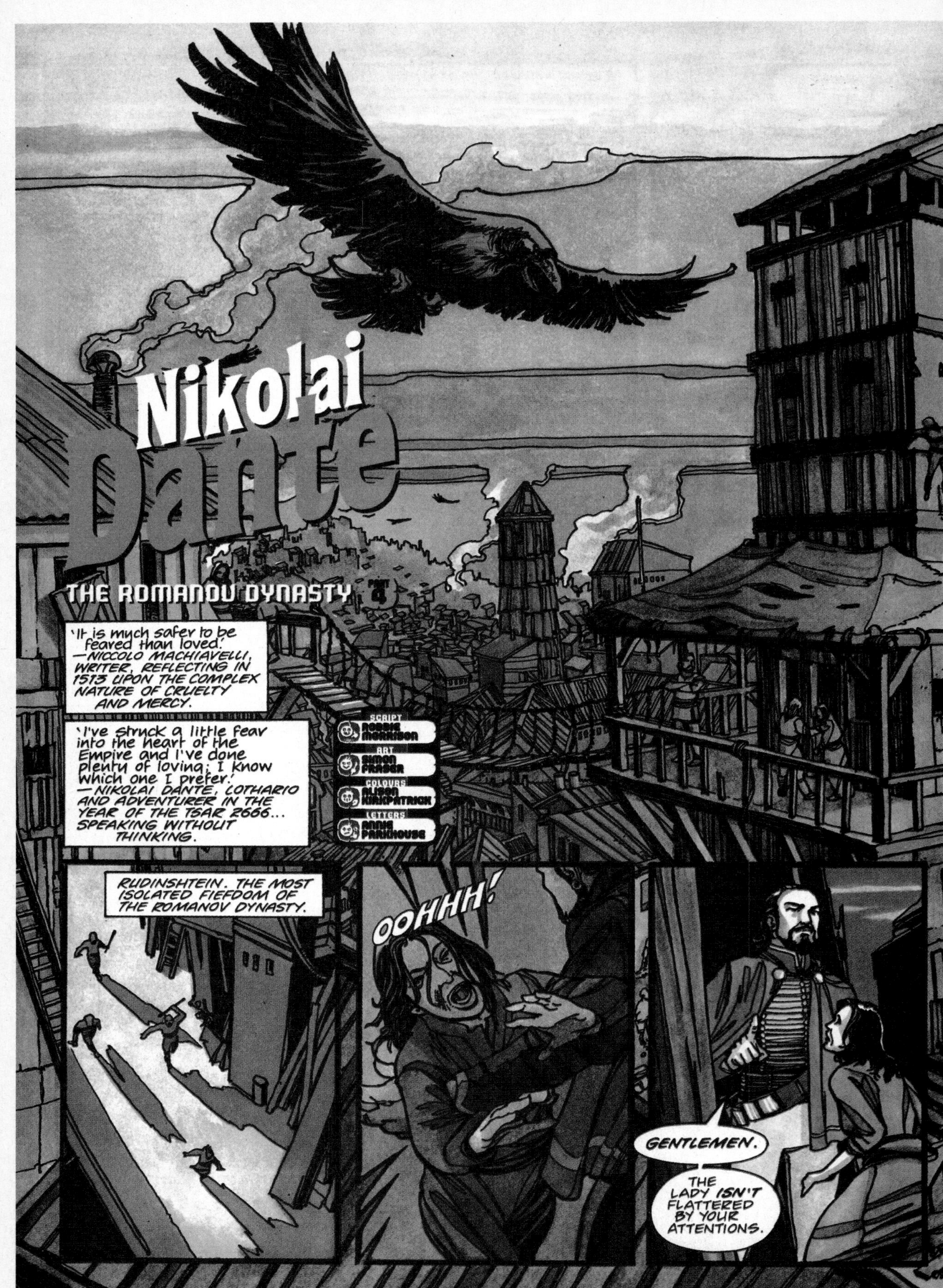
Nikolai Dante
THE ROMANOV DYNASTY
PART 4
'It is much safer to be feared than loved.' —NICCOLO MACHIAVELLI, WRITER, REFLECTING IN 1513 UPON THE COMPLEX NATURE OF CRUELTY AND MERCY.
'I've struck a little fear into the heart of the Empire and I've done plenty of loving; I know which one I prefer.' —NIKOLAI DANTE, COTHARIO AND ADVENTURER IN THE YEAR OF THE TSAR 2666... SPEAKING WITHOUT THINKING.
SCRIPT ROBBIE MORRISON
ART SIMON FRASER
COLOURS ALISON KIRKPATRICK
LETTERS ANNIE PARKHOUSE
RUDINSHTEIN. THE MOST ISOLATED FIEFDOM OF THE ROMANOV DYNASTY.
OOHHH!
GENTLEMEN.
THE LADY ISN'T FLATTERED BY YOUR ATTENTIONS.

LOOKS LIKE ONE OF THE LOCALS HAS FOUND HIMSELF SOME SPIRIT.
THE CHALLENGE'D BE NICE...
ALL THEY'VE BEEN GOOD AT SO FAR IS BEGGING AND DYING!
SORRY--
I'M NOT THE BEGGING TYPE!
!

HHHLLLKKKK!

YOU SHOULDN'T HAVE INTERFERED, STRANGER, NOT FOR ME.
THE KARAZIN ARE ANIMALS. THEY'LL HUNT YOU FOR THIS. THEY'LL KILL YOU.

KILL ME?

I'M TOO COOL TO KILL.
FORGIVE ME, SIRE!
I DIDN'T SEE THE CREST! I DID NOT KNOW YOU WERE OF THE ROMANOV DYNASTY.

WHOA!
GET UP— I'M NOT INTO HUMILITY.

THE NAME'S DANTE. NIKOLAI DANTE.
I'M THE BLACK SHEEP OF THE FAMILY.

THEY'VE LIVED AS OUTLAWS SINCE THE DESTRUCTION OF THEIR DYNASTY, SUPPORTING THEMSELVES BY PRODUCING AND DISTRIBUTING THE DRUG CHERT-DEVIL.

UNDER THEIR LEADER LAZAREV—AN ADDICT TO THE FRENZY OF CHERT—THEY'VE BECOME LITTLE MORE THAN BARBARIANS.

BUSINESS MUST BE BOOMING. THEY RECENTLY OVERWHELMED RUDINSHTEIN AND ENSLAVED THE POPULATION TO INCREASE CHERT PRODUCTION. WE DISPATCHED AN ENVOY, YOUNG ARKADY, TO OFFER THEM TERMS OF SURRENDER.

THEY RESPONDED BY TAKING HIM HOSTAGE. YOU WILL EFFECT HIS RESCUE AND INFORM US WHEN YOU ARE BOTH SAFE. WE WILL DO THE REST.

THE KARAZIN REALLY TORE THIS PLACE APART.
THEIR BASE IS AT THE HEART OF THE CITY—THEY HAVEN'T BEEN HERE.
WHAT LITTLE MAINTENANCE THE GOVERNORS COULD AFFORD WAS CANCELLED WHEN THE ROMANOVS INCREASED THE YEARLY TRIBUTE.

HOW LONG HAVE YOU BEEN WITH THE ROMANOV DYNASTY?
ABOUT A WEEK—THOUGH IT FEELS MORE LIKE TWELVE.
YOU'RE NOT LIKE THEM.

IS THAT A COMPLIMENT OR AN INSULT?
I KNOW WHICH WAY I MEANT IT, SIRE.
MY HUSBAND AND FAMILY ARE AMONGST THE SLAVES TAKEN BY THE KARAZIN.

IF YOU WERE TO FREE THEM... I WOULD BE YOURS.
I KNOW THAT IS ALREADY YOUR RIGHT AS A MEMBER OF THE RULING DYNASTY, BUT—

THAT'S NO ONE'S RIGHT.

WHAT'S YOUR NAME, GIRL?
TAMARA.
I'LL FREE YOUR FAMILY, TAMARA. I'LL FREE ALL THE SLAVES.

Virtuous behaviour from *you* is most unexpected, Dante.

Perhaps we'll make a *gentleman* of you, yet? Or perhaps your elevation to the *aristocracy* has merely raised your tastes above the gutter?

SHUT UP, CREST.

HAVE YOU LOCATED THE ROMANOV ENVOY, YET?

Genescan confirms that he's imprisoned under heavy guard in a ShantyScraper on the opposite side of the Karazin camp from us.

NATALIA

Navigating the massed forces of the enemy, however, may prove a little *troublesome*.

Perhaps you should have added, *'Or die trying,'* to that reckless promise about freeing slaves.

Diavolo...

NEXT PROG >> **BASTARD OF THE FAMILY!**

NIKOLAI DANTE IS NOW A MEMBER OF THE ROMANOV DYNASTY, THANKS TO THE SENTIENT WEAPONS BIO-CREST BONDED TO HIS BODY.
DANTE IS SENT TO THE DISTANT FIEFDOM OF RUDINSHTEIN WHICH HAS BEEN OVERWHELMED BY THE ONCE NOBLE KARAZIN DYNASTY.
DANTE'S MISSION IS TO FREE A ROMANOV ENVOY CALLED ARKADY HELD CAPTIVE BY THE KARAZIN...
Nikolai Dante
THE ROMANOV DYNASTY
ROBBIE MORRISON
SIMON FRASER
ALISON KIRKPATRICK
ANNIE PARKHOUSE
THEN THERE WAS THE GROZNY GANG...
MY BROTHER KONSTANTIN FUSED THEM INTO ONE MASS AGAINST THE HULL OF THEIR STARSHIP.
IT NOW TAKES PRIDE OF PLACE AMONGST OUR FAMILY TAPESTRIES.
THEIR SCREAMING, MELTED FACES AND CONTORTED LIMBS ARE THE TOAST OF THE ART WORLD.
SHUT UP, BOY, OR YOU'LL BE A CORPSE, NOT A CAPTIVE.

FOR ALL THE OSTENTATIOUS METHODS OF ELIMINATING ENEMIES...

THE SIMPLEST ONES ARE SOMETIMES THE BEST.

For the record, Dante, I must state that I did not advise a frontal assault.

BACK-DOOR ENTRIES AREN'T MY STYLE, CREST.

YOU RESCUED ME FROM THE KARAZIN, BUT WHO'S GOING TO RESCUE YOU FROM ME?

YOU BEAR THE CREST UNDER FALSE PRETENCES, STRANGER.
I WAS TO HAVE RECEIVED MY BIRTHRIGHT WEAPONS CREST BEFORE COMING HERE. SOMEONE— YOU—INTERCEPTED IT IN TRANSIT.

THIS WAS TO HAVE BEEN MY FIRST MISSION FOR THE DYNASTY. FIRST BLOOD.
I SHOULD KILL YOU FOR ROBBING ME OF THAT HONOUR.

WHOOMPH!
YOU'VE HAD YOUR FIRST BLOOD...

THERE'S A CITY FULL OF THIEVES AND MURDERERS OUT THERE WAITING TO DO THE SAME...
AND IF YOU WANT TO TRY SPILLING MINE, GET IN LINE!

LAZAREV!
LAZAREV!

THE ENTERTAINMENT'S ABOUT TO COMMENCE...
WHAT?

'EACH NIGHT, LAZAREV, THE KARAZIN LEADER, FORCES SLAVES TO ENGAGE HIM IN COMBAT.'
LAZAREV!
LAZAREV!

I'M GIVING YOU AN OPPORTUNITY YOU DON'T DESERVE.
LIVE LIKE SLAVES—OR DIE LIKE FREE MEN.

WEAPONS.

CHERT.

GGRRRAAAA!

LAZAREV'S ADDICTED TO CHERT, THE DRUG THE KARAZIN MANUFACTURE.
THE DUELS FEED HIS HABIT, SPEEDING THE DRUG'S PROGRESS THROUGH HIS SYSTEM.

'THERE'S NOTHING LIKE THE THRILL OF THE KILL TO GET THE BLOOD PUMPING.'

GIVE THE ORDER TO ATTACK NOW.
I WANT TO WATCH SOME REAL BLOOD-SPORTS.
NO!
WE HAVE TO FREE THE SLAVES FIRST.

WHAT!? WE DON'T FIGHT FOR THEM. THEY FIGHT FOR US.
THEY'RE OURS TO DO WITH AS WE PLEASE.

I MADE A PROMISE.
GET YOURSELF TO SAFETY AND GIVE ME TWENTY MINUTES, THEN ORDER THE ATTACK.

PROMISES ARE FOR BREAKING.
ARKADY ROMANOV TO DYNASTY COMMAND. LAUNCH EAGLESTRIKE NOW.

AND THEY CALL ME THE BASTARD OF THE FAMILY!

NEXT PROG ▸ MORE ABOUT THE ART OF DIPLOMACY!

SCRIPT ROBBIE MORRISON
ART SIMON FRASER
COLOURS ALISON KIRKPATRICK
LETTERS ANNIE PARKHOUSE

NIKOLAI DANTE IS IN THE DISTANT ROMANOV FIEFDOM OF **RUDINSHTEIN**, WHICH HAS BEEN OVERWHELMED BY THE DRUG-DEALING, DECADENT **KARAZIN** DYNASTY.

DANTE RESCUES A ROMANOV ENVOY AND **FREES** THE KARAZIN **SLAVES** BUT THEIR ESCAPE IS BLOCKED...

TAKE THE **ROMANOV** FIRST!

Nikolai Dante

THE ROMANOV DYNASTY

PART 6

GGGNNHH!

Dante! The odds against surviving this unnecessary encounter are astronomical!

QUOTE ME ODDS WHEN I'M GAMBLING WITH MONEY, CREST!
NOT WITH MY LIFE!

UUUHH!

YOU'VE A TALENT FOR TROUBLE, LITTLE BROTHER.
IF WE WERE ALL LIKE YOU, THE ROMANOVS WOULD BE A VERY SHORT-LIVED DYNASTY.

FROM THE FILES OF THE RAVEN CORPS:
KONSTANTIN: Sophisticated and Charming. A born leader. A born killer. A born everything.
CREST CAPABILITIES: The ability to generate fusion energy comparable to the greatest Imperial war machines from within his own body.
SAY HELLO TO THE REST OF THE FAMILY—AND FAREWELL TO THE KARAZIN.
LULU: A terrifying seductive beauty who has driven the strongest Imperial subjects to suicide and insanity.
CREST CAPABILITIES: The creation of cybernetic entities which devour their prey in insect-like swarms.
Fuoco...

VIKTOR: The lone wolf of the Romanovs. Dwells in isolation, shunning even the company of his siblings unless necessary.
CREST CAPABILITIES: Unknown. No Imperial agent has ever dared investigate him.
ANDREAS: Incorrigible adventurer and philandering seducer of widows and heiresses.
CREST CAPABILITIES: Bio-blades which generate an energy-field of variable size. Rumoured to have once decapitated 27 men with a single blade.
NASTASIA: The Romanov Bitch. Narcissistic and coquettish. Habitual killer of anyone less admiring of her looks than she is herself.
CREST CAPABILITIES: The transmutation of bodily fluids into venomous or acidic substances.

THIS IS NOT A PROPOSITION, LAZAREV—YOU HAVE NO CHOICE IN THE MATTER.
CONTINUE CHERT PRODUCTION, BUT HAND OVER ALL PROFITS TO US. IN RETURN, YOU WILL BE GIVEN RUDINSHTEIN TO RULE AS YOU SEE FIT.

Tamara...

I TOLD YOU IT WOULD BE FUN TO WATCH...

NO!

LOOK WHAT HE DID TO THESE PEOPLE!
YOU CAN'T JUST GIVE THEM TO HIM!

LORD KONSTANTIN, I PLEDGE UNDYING LOYALTY TO THE ROMANOV DYNASTY.
THAT'S THE SPIRIT.

IT'S CALLED DIPLOMACY.
RUDINSHTEIN FEARS LAZAREV, LAZAREV FEARS US—WHAT BETTER WAY TO KEEP ORDER?

NEXT PROG ⊳ HEROES DIE YOUNG...

Evasive action, Dante! Evasive action!
RELAX CREST, I'VE GOT HIS MEASURE...
Nikolai Dante
NIKOLAI DANTE IS IN THE DISTANT ROMANOV FIEFDOM OF RUDINSHTEIN, A POOR PROVINCE CONTROLLED BY THE DRUG-DEALING, DECADENT KARAZIN DYNASTY.
DANTE IS FIGHTING A DUEL TO THE DEATH WITH THE KARAZIN LEADER LAZAREV. THE BATTLE IS WATCHED BY DANTE'S ROMANOV SIBLINGS...

WWOOAARRGH!
Fool!

Lazarev is addicted to Chert, the most powerful stimulative substance known to humanity. It raises psycho-physical sensations to an orgiastic frenzy!
GIVE ME THAT IN SCUMBAG LANGUAGE...

THE ROMANOV DYNASTY
He enjoys pain!

AAAGH-KKK!!

His strike fractured every rib on your left side — shield yourself from further attack.
EA-EASY FOR YOU TO SAY...

SCRIPT
ROBBIE MORRISON
ART
SIMON FRASER
COLOURS
ALISON KIRKPATRICK
LETTERS
ANNIE PARKHOUSE

Dante...
I KNOW!
I KNOW!

EVASIVE ACTION!

Evasive action usually means getting yourself out of danger, not deeper into it...

OOHFFF!

AKK!?

I THINK WE GOT HIM, CREST...

HEH.
I think not...

GGRRRAAAA!

HAAAH!

HUHH!?
PAINFUL ENOUGH?
STILL ENJOYING YOURSELF?

HEH HEH HEH

GRRAAAAAggqkkk!!

FUOCO...
HE'S DEAD NOW...

Famous last words, thief...

Now why couldn't you have done that at the very start?
cough... shut up, crest...

I'D SAY OUR BASTARD BROTHER PULLED THAT OFF WITH A CERTAIN AMOUNT OF CRUDE STYLE.
HE MOANS WELL. I PREFER A MAN TO WHIMPER, BUT HE MOANS WELL.
SURELY IT'S KINDEST TO KILL HIM NOW— SAVE THE DYNASTY FURTHER EMBARRASSMENT.

KONSTANTIN? KILL HIM?

IT MIGHT NOT BE THAT EASY.
DANTE!
DANTE!
DANTE!

WHEN WAS THE LAST TIME ANYONE CHEERED FOR THE ROMANOV DYNASTY WITHOUT A GUN AT THEIR HEAD?

SOMETIMES IT **PAYS** TO HAVE A **HERO** IN THE FAMILY.
WHAT DO **YOU** SAY TO THAT, **LITTLE BROTHER?**

NEXT PROG ▶ PATERNAL INSTINCTS!

THE ROMANOV WINTER PALACE, WHERE NIKOLAI DANTE IS NURSING THE WOUNDS SUFFERED DURING HIS FIRST MISSION AS THE NEW MEMBER OF THE ROMANOV DYNASTY...
AAOOWWW!
Nikolai Dante
THE ROMANOV DYNASTY
SCRIPT ROBBIE MORRISON
ART SIMON FRASER
COLOURS ALISON KIRKPATRICK
LETTERS ANNIE PARKHOUSE

WHOA! WHOA!
COULD YOU MOVE OVER JUST A LITTLE?
THIS IS SILLY— I TOLD YOU YOU WEREN'T UP TO IT, YET.

UP TO IT?
IF WE CAN GET IT TOGETHER JUST A LITTLE BIT MORE...

YOU'LL FIND THAT'S FAR FROM THE CASE...

OOOHH!
HUHH!?

WHOA!
BY ANASTASIA'S BONES! THE UNIT GYROSCOPE—

—IS UNDER MY CONTROL, GIRL.
GET OUT. FROM NOW ON YOUNG NIKOLAI WILL BE ATTENDED ONLY BY MALE MEDICS.
YES, LORD DMITRI.

WHEN YOU CAME TO US, I TOLD YOU THAT BEARING THE CREST AND BEING WORTHY OF IT WERE ENTIRELY DIFFERENT THINGS.

I'M BEGINNING TO WONDER WHETHER YOU EVEN WANT TO BE WORTHY...

YOU INITIATED A DUEL WITH LAZAREV IN DEFIANCE OF A DYNASTIC DECREE TO INSTALL HIM AS PUPPET GOVERNOR OF RUDINSHTEIN. WHY?
HE WOULD HAVE DESTROYED THEM. HE WAS A TYRANT, A BARBARIAN...

MANY SAY THE SAME OF ME.
I VIEW IT AS COMPLIMENTARY, A TESTAMENT TO ROMANOV POWER AND AUTHORITY.

I DID IT FOR POWER...
TO PROVE I'M MORE THAN JUST THE BASTARD SON OF THE ROMANOV DYNASTY.

PROVE IT TO WHO? YOURSELF? TO PROVE YOU'RE BETTER THAN US, PERHAPS?
SINCE WINNING RUDINSHTEIN, YOU'VE LOWERED THEIR TAXES, INTRODUCED BENEFICIAL REFORMS...

LOWERING THEIR TAXES LETS THEM GENERATE NEW WEALTH, GIVES THEM STABILITY AND SECURITY.
EVERYBODY SAYS I'M A THIEF— I'LL ROB THEM BLIND LATER.

NEVER LET THEM LOVE YOU— IT'S EASY TO HURT THE THINGS YOU LOVE.
MAKE THEM FEAR YOU. FEAR IS THE KEY.

HEY...
I CAN BE SCARY...

NO, BOY, YOU CAN'T!
YOU DON'T HAVE THE KILLING IN YOU!

AND WITHOUT THE KILLING, YOU'RE ONLY FIT FOR KILLING!

WHY DO YOU THINK I'M HERE?

IT'S JUDGMENT DAY, YOUNG NIKOLAI.

SHAME REALLY. I'VE GROWN FOND OF YOUR UNPREDICTABILITY IN THE WAY A HORSEMAN FEELS TOWARDS A STEED HE MUST BREAK.
SADLY, UNPREDICTABILITY IN THE RANKS IS SOMETHING NO IMPERIAL DYNASTY CAN AFFORD.

THE THIEVES' WORLD HAS LEFT ITS MARK ON YOU. I THINK YOU'RE TOO MUCH YOUR OWN MAN TO EVER BE TRUSTED.
PERHAPS IF WE'D HAD YOU SINCE BIRTH...

HOW IS YOUR MOTHER? I KNOW YOU'VE BEEN CHECKING DYNASTY RECORDS TO SEE WHICH OF US KNEW HER.
STILL REIVING THE EMPIRE FOR ALL SHE'S WORTH?

I HAVEN'T SEEN HER IN OVER 10 YEARS.
SHE ABANDONED ME...

SHE WAS QUITE A WOMAN. FIERY, ARROGANT, TREACHEROUS...
I HAD TO BREAK HER IN SOME WAY...

WHAT?

YOU DIDN'T THINK YOU WERE CONCEIVED OUT OF LOVE, DID YOU?

BASTARD!

I'M AFRAID *YOU*'RE THE ONLY ONE THAT INSULT APPLIES TO...

ALL ROMANOVS BEAR THE CREST...

YOU THINK I'D GIVE THAT PACK OF *WOLVES* I SIRED WEAPONS THEY CAN DESTROY ME WITH?

STILL THINK YOU'RE WORTHY, YOUNG NIKOLAI?
CAN YOU ACCEPT THE KILLING!?

...kill you...
I'LL KILL YOU...

HA HA HA HA HA!

YOU WOULD IF YOU COULD. ALL MY CHILDREN WOULD. I BRED IT INTO THEM.
RUTHLESSNESS. AMBITION. THAT'S WHAT GIVES US OUR POWER, MAKES THE TSAR FEAR US. NOT THE WEAPONS CRESTS.

REST EASY, NIKOLAI DANTE.
WE'LL MAKE A ROMANOV OUT OF YOU, YET.

BOJEMOI...

WELCOME TO THE FAMILY...
THE END

RUSSIA'S GREATEST LOVE MACHINE

Script: Robbie Morrison

Art: Chris Weston

Letters: Annie Parkhouse

Originally published in *2000 AD* Prog 1066

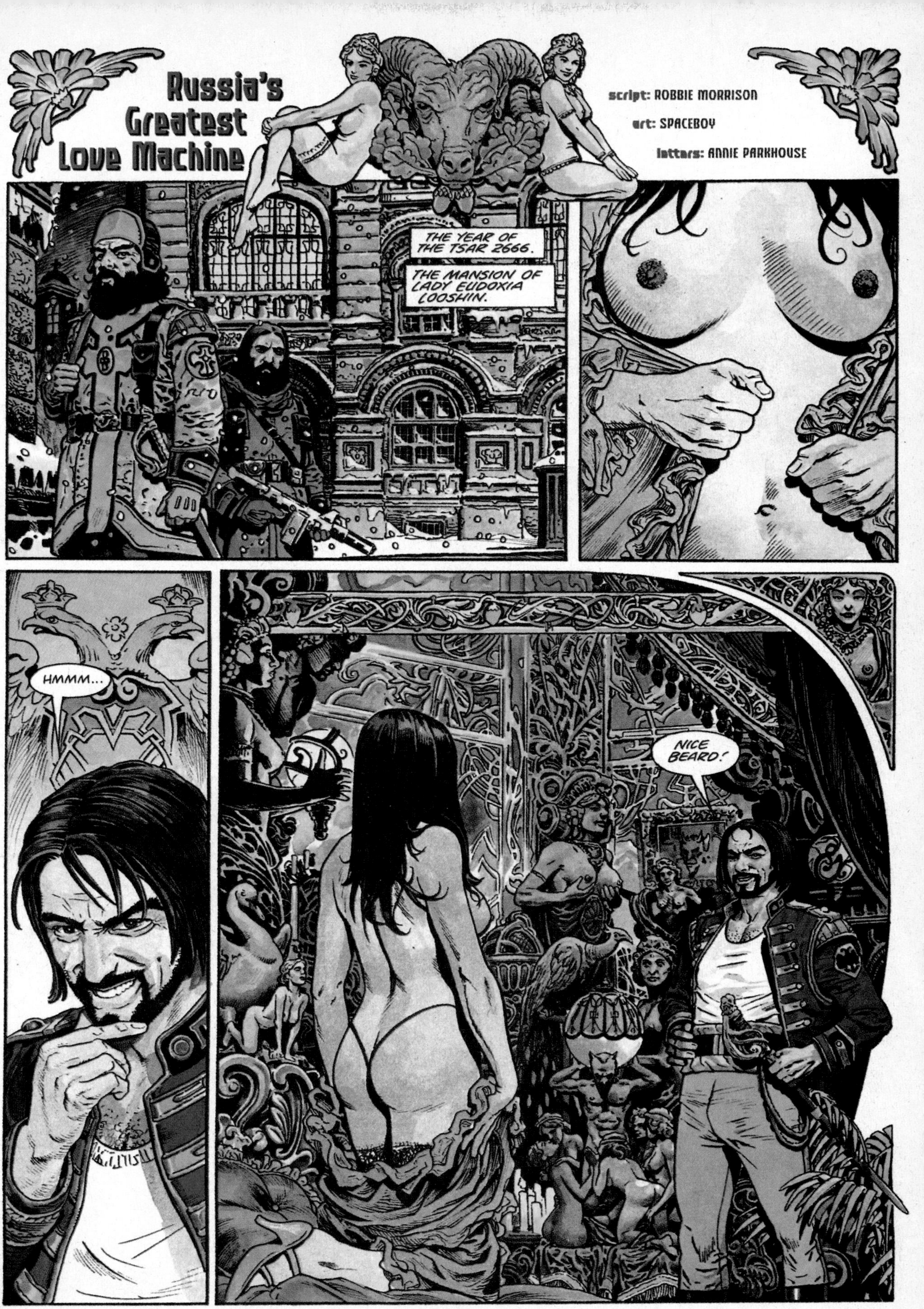

Russia's Greatest Love Machine

script: ROBBIE MORRISON

art: SPACEBOY

letters: ANNIE PARKHOUSE

THE YEAR OF THE TSAR 2666.

THE MANSION OF LADY EUDOXIA LOOSHIN.

HMMM...

NICE BEARD!

THANK YOU.
I TRIM IT MYSELF.
The Devil's Marturs are an Imperial Cult fanatically devoted to the hedonistic Grigori Rasputin, the infamous Mad Monk, whose corrupt influence over the last Tsar of the First Empire contributed to its downfall many centuries ago.
Sex with the Devil's Marturs is reputed to be an experience of the wildest excess.
Ladu Eudoxia Looshin, a disciple of legendary decadence, has waulaid Nikolai Dante with the intention of testing his ladukiller reputation to the limit.
My morally deficient 'master' would normally relish the challenge. however, as a sign of devotion to the hirsute Rasputin, all Devil's Marturs sport beards — even the women.
KISS ME, NIKOLAI!
Thick, full, heavu, manlu beards.
KISS ME!
WHOA! WHOA! SORRY!
I, UH, JUST NEED TO GO TO THE TOILET! DESPERATELY!

GET A GRIP OF YOURSELF!
SHE'S A BEAUTIFUL WOMAN! BEAUTIFUL, BUXOM, SWEET AND SEXY—JUST A WEE BIT HAIRY.
Surely you don't judge beauty on a depilatory scale? A man of your experience must have been with hirsute women before.
ARMPITS, FINE! LEGS, WHAT THE HELL! BUT, BUT—SHE'S GOT A BUSHIER BEARD THAN ME!

Her beard has obviously awakened your homophobia. Or perhaps something deeper?
Perhaps you're scared you'll enjoy it? If you can kiss a bearded woman, why not a man?

IF YOU WEREN'T BONDED TO ME, CREST, I'D RUN YOU THROUGH FOR THAT!
I'M HETERO FROM HEAD TO TOE—AND I'LL PROVE IT!

GET READY FOR SOME LOVING, MILADY!
I'M COMING IN HOT AND HARD!

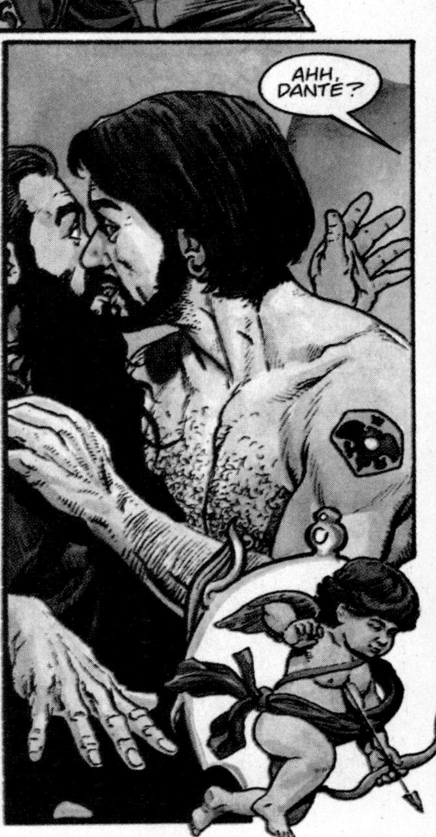
AHH, DANTE?

I SEE YOU'VE INTRODUCED YOURSELF TO MY BUTLER, IVAN.

GOOD EVENING, SIR.
EEUUGH!
IT MIGHT BE PRUDENT IF I LEFT NOW, MADAM.
YOU MAY FEEL THE NEED OF THIS, SIR.

I'M DISAPPOINTED, NIKOLAI.
YOUR REPUTATION AS A LADIES' MAN SEEMS TO HAVE BEEN EXAGGERATED. I'D HAVE THOUGHT YOU MORE OPEN-MINDED.
EXAGGERATED, MILADY!? I'M COOLER THAN CASANOVA AND RANDIER THAN RASPUTIN!
WHEN THE DEVIL'S MARTYRS ARE DEAD AND BURIED, DANTE'S DISCIPLES'LL STILL BE HAVING A HELL OF A TIME!

AS FOR OPEN-MINDED, I JUST SNOGGED YOUR BUTLER!

I FINALLY GET YOU WHERE I WANT YOU.
YEAH, LET'S GET IT ON AND BUMP SOME BRISTLES TOGETHER.

WEIRD HOW YOUR BEARD ITCHES DURING MOMENTS OF PASSION...
MUST BE ALL THAT STATIC ELECTRICITY...
RA-RA-RASPUTIN, RUSSIA'S GREATEST LOVE MACHINE, THERE WAS A CAT WHO REALLY WAS COOL.
Are you always so happy creeping out of ladies' bedchambers like a thief in the night?
LOVE 'EM AND LEAVE 'EM, CREST, THAT'S THE WAY OF THE THIEVES' WORLD— AND RELIEVE THEM OF THEIR JEWELLRY TOO, IF YOU CAN.
BESIDES, I COULDN'T LAST ANOTHER 10 ROUNDS, MY FACE IS KILLING ME.
IT'S USUALLY ME WHO LEAVES GIRLS WITH STUBBLE BURNS!
THE END

THE GENTLEMAN THIEF

Script: Robbie Morrison

Art: Simon Fraser

Colors: Alison Kirkpatrick

Letters: Annie Parkhouse

Originally published in *2000 AD* Progs 1067-1070

Nikolai Dante

THE GENTLEMAN THIEF PART 1

SCRIPT ROBBIE MORRISON
ART SIMON FRASER
COLOURS ALISON KIRKPATRICK
LETTERS ANNIE PARKHOUSE

HOTEL YALTA, PLEASURE RESORT OF THE IMPERIAL ARISTOCRACY, STRETCHING ALONG THE ENTIRE COASTLINE OF THE BLACK SEA.

'Every so often, the aristocracy produces an individual whose unashamed embrace of hedonism rivals the infamous decadence of the First Empire.'
'Not since the divorce of Andreas Romanov and Epiphany Zakamenny has the Hotel Yalta seen a party of this magnitude, now in its third week and showing no signs of abating.'
'Fortuitously or not, the name of Romanov is also associated with this celebration, for the host is none other than the bastard son of the Romanov Dynasty—Nikolai Dante, the Hero of Rudinshtein, whose idea of recuperating from injuries received in his last duel would kill most able-bodied men.'—THE IMPERIAL TIMES.
I'LL SHOW YOU MINE IF YOU SHOW ME YOURS.
YOU FIRST.

BOJEMOI!

YOU DON'T THINK IT'S A TRIFLE OSTENTATIOUS, DO YOU?
ON THE CONTRARY, I THINK THEY'RE MAGNIFICENT.

I WAS TALKING ABOUT MY TATTOO.
I KNOW.

SIR! THE HOTEL SEEMS TO HAVE MADE A MISTAKE.
YOU ARE OCCUPYING OUR ROOMS, THOUGH I'M SURE YOU'LL SOON VACATE THEM IN THE NAME OF THE TSAR.

MISTAKE? I DOUBT IT.
ROOMS AT THE YALTA ARE USUALLY ALLOCATED BY THE SIZE OF A MAN'S POUCH.

MONEY POUCH, THAT IS.
I WOULDN'T WANT TO MAKE YOU FEEL ANY MORE INADEQUATE THAN YOU ALREADY ARE.

WHAT'S YOUR NAME, YOU ARROGANT SWINE?
DANTE.
NIKOLAI DANTE.

I'M CAPTAIN ARBATOV OF THE TSAR'S LIGHTHORSEMEN.
ONE OF MY BROTHERS WAS SKINNED ALIVE BECAUSE OF YOU, ANOTHER HURLED FROM THE WINTER PALACE.

IT'S A PLEASURE TO MAKE YOUR ACQUAINTANCE!

Y'KNOW, CAPTAIN...
YOUR FAMILY AND I ARE GOING TO HAVE TO STOP MEETING LIKE THIS...

IT'S BAD FOR YOUR HEALTH!

YOU'LL PAY FOR THAT, ROMANOV DOG!

COOL!
THE ONLY THING THE PARTY'S MISSING IS A GOOD BRAWL!

HALT!
ANY FURTHER AGGRESSION WILL BE REPAID IN KIND!
SECURITY

THE HOTEL YALTA IS NEUTRAL TERRITORY, GENTLEMEN, FREE OF IMPERIAL DISPUTES OR DYNASTIC INTRIGUE—BY ORDER OF THE TSAR.
WE ARE BUSINESSMEN, AND ANYTHING OR ANYONE DISRUPTING BUSINESS WILL NOT BE TOLERATED.

BUT, LORD KONIGSBERG, DANTE—
ULLURRKK!
ANYTHING OR ANYONE, CAPTAIN. YOU AND YOUR MEN WILL BE GIVEN OTHER ROOMS. DO NOT ABUSE OUR HOSPITALITY AGAIN.

A WORD OF ADVICE TO THE HIGH SPENDERS AMONGST YOU.
THE YALTA INDULGES YOUR EVERY PLEASURE, BUT ALWAYS REMEMBER OUR MOTTO...

NO ONE HERE GETS OUT ALIVE WITHOUT PAYING THEIR BILL...
NIKOLAI DANTE.

YOU HAVE A COMMUNICATION FROM THE WINTER PALACE.
PROBABLY THE FAMILY TELLING ME TO SPEND MORE MONEY—THEY MUST BE EMBARRASSED AT HOW CHEAPLY I'M LIVING.

LULU! YOU'RE LOOKING ESPECIALLY VAMPISH TODAY!
HOW'RE THINGS BACK AT THE HUMBLE FAMILY HOME?
ALL THE BETTER FOR YOUR ABSENCE, LITTLE BROTHER. SHAME THEY CAN'T STAY THAT WAY.

NEXT PROG ⏩ THE MARK OF DANTE!

YOUR MONEY OR YOUR LIFE!

'The incorrigible Nikolai Dante found himself penniless in the Hotel Yalta, whose motto, "No one here gets out alive without paying their bill," was brutally enforced.'

'There was only one option — thievery.' FROM 'BRIGANDS OF THE EMPIRE,' BY MARIA BERIA.

WHOA! DANGLEBERRIES!
PULL YOUR PANTS UP, CARDASS!

YOU IMPUDENT DOG! MY PERSONAL HYGIENE IS BEYOND REPROACH!
I'LL RUN YOU THROUGH LIKE I DID COUNT VRONSKY IN THE BATTLE OF VOLKA CREEK.

WOOAARGH!

MY THANKS, SIR.
I WAS ABOUT TO TAKE A SIMILAR COURSE OF ACTION MYSELF.

THE GENTLEMAN THIEF, MILADY, THAT'S ME.

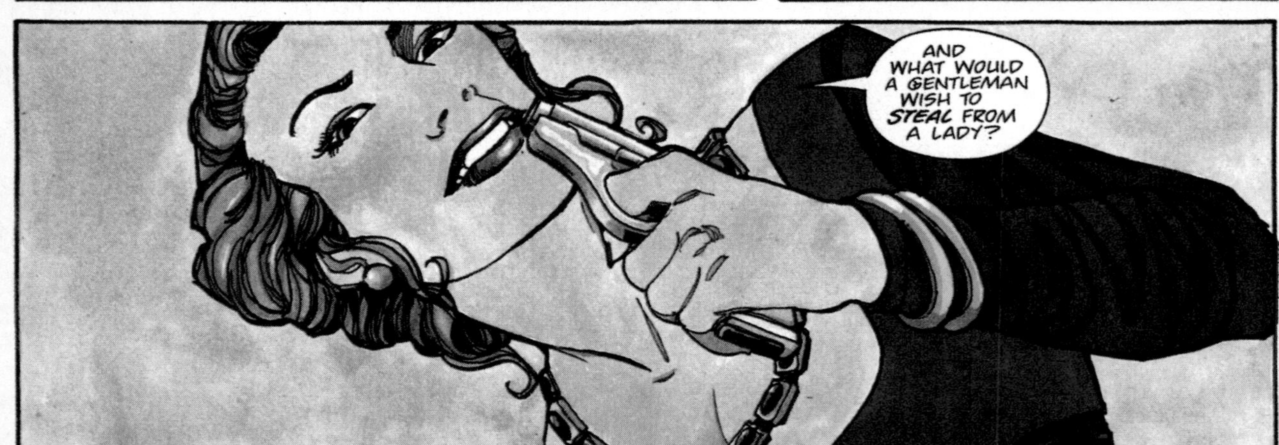
AND WHAT WOULD A GENTLEMAN WISH TO STEAL FROM A LADY?

ONLY A KISS FROM THOSE SWEET LIPS.
I SHOULD WEAR A MASK MORE OFTEN, IT WORKS WONDERS WITH THE LADIES.
THAT'S THE TENTH SET OF TONSILS I'VE TICKLED TONIGHT, THOUGH THEY WERE DEFINITELY THE TASTIEST.
'The Hotel Yalta is definitely the place to be. In addition to an ongoing party of epic magnitude, it has become the target of a daring Gentleman Thief.'
'In just a few short days, the brigand has set the public imagination racing and earned himself a small fortune...
'...not to mention an astronomical price on his head, courtesy of the Yalta's enraged owners.' — THE IMPERIAL TIMES.
BOJEMOI!

CREST!
YOU'RE SUPPOSED TO BE DISRUPTING THEIR SCANNERS SO THEY CAN'T FIND ME!
I am, but I can't make you invisible.

If you insist on massaging your ego by hanging around posing in plain sight, how can they possibly not find you?

'The Thief delights in goading his pursuers into spectacular rooftop pursuits, then vanishes like a phantom just when capture seems inevitable.'
— THE IMPERIAL TIMES.

GUNHAWK 7 TO YALTA COMMAND. WE'VE LOST HIM— AGAIN!

YOU RANDY ROGUE!

'Noblewomen from all over the Empire are rumoured to be journeying to the Yalta in the hope of having their favours stolen by this dashing adventurer.' — THE IMPERIAL TIMES.
YOU'VE COME TO RAVISH ME, HAVEN'T YOU, SIR. RAVISH ME AND STEAL MY MONEY.

THE MONEY WOULD BE FINE, AS FOR THE RAVISHING...
IT'S BEEN A LONG NIGHT, I DON'T KNOW IF I'M UP TO IT.
UP TO IT!
YOU'VE A WICKED TONGUE, YOU BAWDY FELLOW!

I'LL DEFEND MY MONEY AS VALIANTLY AS MY HONOUR — YOU'LL HAVE TO TAKE THEM FROM ME.
JANGLE!

IT'S ALRIGHT, REALLY. KEEP THEM. I'LL BE OFF.
JINGLE!
YOU CAN'T TRICK ME, YOU SCOUNDREL. YOU'VE BEEN UNDRESSING ME WITH YOUR EYES SINCE YOU ARRIVED!

SHAMELESSLY CARESSING MY RIPE FLESH WITH THEM.
UH. OVER-RIPE, ACTUALLY. FIT TO BURST, IN FACT.

UNHAND ME, YOU RUFFIAN!
MMMPH!

I'M NOT SOME TAME STEED YOU CAN CASUALLY MOUNT!
BOJEMOI!

NEXT PROG ▷ TO CATCH A THIEF!

WHAT'S GOING ON, KONIGSBERG? THE YALTA'S SUPPOSED TO BE NEUTRAL TERRITORY, YET YOU'RE LETTING ARBATOV PURSUE HIS VENDETTA AGAINST ME?

NOT AT ALL, DANTE. I'M MERELY ENFORCING OUR ONLY LAW.

NO ONE HERE GETS OUT ALIVE WITHOUT PAYING THEIR BILL!

SCRIPT ROBBIE MORRISON
ART SIMON FRASER
COLOURS ALISON KIRKPATRICK
LETTERS ANNIE PARKHOUSE

CAPTAIN ARBATOV HAS FORMULATED A MOST INTERESTING THEORY AROUND YOU.
FOR THE LAST MONTH, DANTE, YOU'VE BEEN THROWING THE BIGGEST PARTY IN THE HISTORY OF THE YALTA, SEEMINGLY AT THE EXPENSE OF THE ROMANOV DYNASTY.
HOWEVER...

AN EXAMINATION OF ROMANOV STATECRAFT REVEALS THAT THE WEALTH OF THE DYNASTIC ELITE IS DRAWN FROM THE LAND THEY OWN.
WHATEVER THEY SPEND IS DEDUCTED FROM THESE FIEFDOMS— NOT NORMALLY A PROBLEM, FOR THEIR HOLDINGS ARE EXTENSIVE.

YOU, HOWEVER, ARE THE GOVERNOR OF RUDINSHTEIN, THE POOREST CITY IN THE EMPIRE.
I HADN'T EVEN HEARD OF IT WHEN I BEGAN MY INVESTIGATION.

YOU'VE ALREADY SPENT ENOUGH TO BANKRUPT RUDINSHTEIN SEVERAL TIMES OVER.
THE ROMANOVS ARE NOT RENOWNED FOR THEIR TOLERANCE— A CITY WHICH NO LONGER PROFITED THEM WOULD BE SEVERELY PUNISHED.

DANTE HAS OBVIOUSLY RESORTED TO THIEVERY IN AN ATTEMPT TO PAY HIS HOTEL BILL AND SAVE HIS CITY FROM SLAUGHTER OR SLAVERY.

I REST MY CASE.

AND VERY ENTERTAINING IT WAS TOO, THOUGH PERSONALLY I'D HAVE SPICED IT UP WITH A LITTLE SEX AND VIOLENCE.

YOU HAVE MY THANKS, CAPTAIN.
YOUR THANKS, THIEF?
I DIDN'T TAKE YOU FOR THE PENITENT SORT.

PENITENCE BE DAMNED. I'M JUST GLAD YOU GAVE ME THE CHANCE TO DO THIS...

AAAGH-KK!

THAT WASN'T AN ADMISSION OF GUILT, LORD KONIGSBERG, IT WAS AN EXPRESSION OF INNOCENCE.
SUBDUE HIM, ENFORCERS!

SECURITY
YALTA
The balcony, Dante. It's the easiest escape route...

THE EASIEST!?

WE'RE ON THE 110TH FLOOR!

GGGNNHH!

DON'T JUST STAND THERE, FOOLS...
FIRE!!

NICE SHOOTING, BOYS!
KEEP IT UP!
HHHLLKK!

YOU SHOT YOUR OWN MEN, ARBATOV.
NOT TO WORRY, THEY WERE ONLY CONSCRIPTS.

CAPTAIN!
THANKS FOR THE GETAWAY VEHICLE!

WHOA!

THE STEEDS ARE BIO-LINKED TO THEIR PILOTS. IT TAKES HOURS TO BREAK THE CODE—AND SECONDS TO REACH THE GROUND!
I HOPE YOUR CAMERAS CATCH HIS FALL. THE TSAR WILL PAY HANDSOMELY TO SEE NIKOLAI DANTE SPLATTERED OVER—

NO!
IT'S NOT POSSIBLE!

HAHAHAHAHA!

I COULD'VE USED YOU BEFORE I JOINED THE ARISTOCRACY, CREST—HOTWIRING HARDWARE WAS NEVER A TALENT OF MINE.

It's not exactly what I was designed for either.
RELAX. ENJOY THE RIDE.
I'VE BEEN RUNNING FROM THE LAW SINCE I WAS OLD ENOUGH TO WALK.

Then it's truly a wonder you ever reached puberty...
BOJEMOI!
GUNHAWKS!

Get out of the air, Dante, we're too easy a target—the GunHawks outclass us in speed, manoeuvrability and firepower.

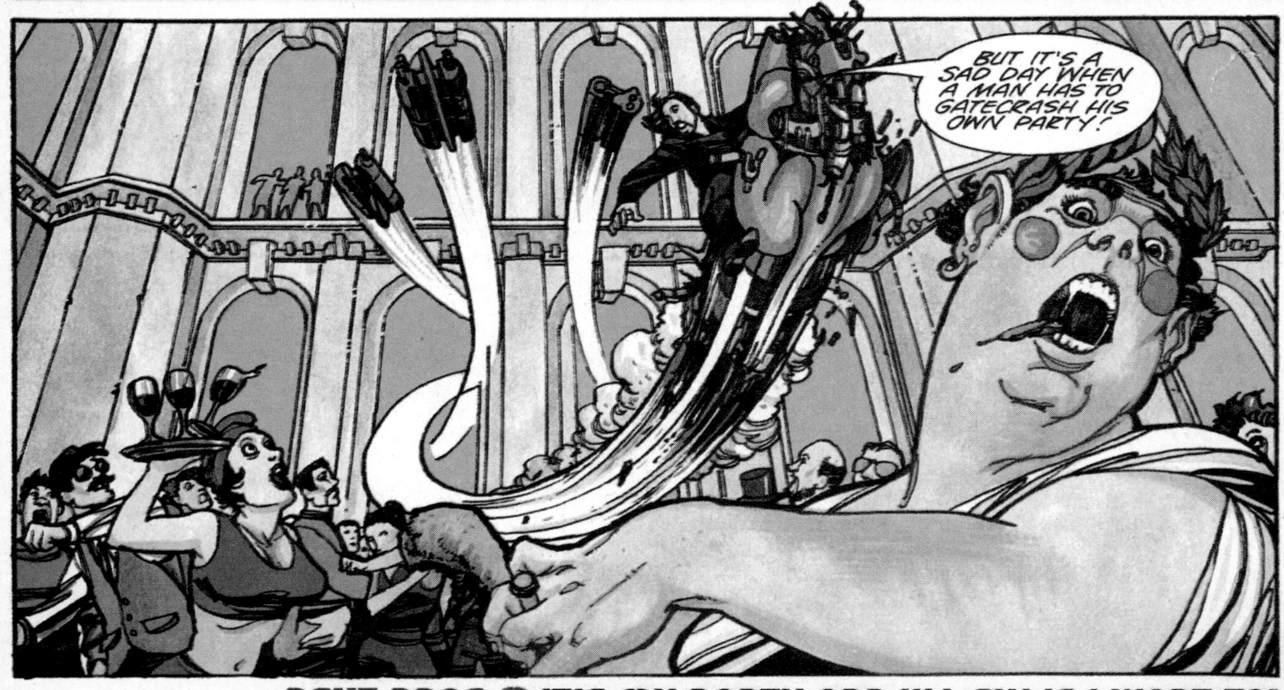

NEXT PROG ⏩ IT'S MY PARTY AND I'LL FLY IF I WANT TO!

THIS IS AN OUTRAGE, YOU YOUNG ROGUE!
I, GENERAL SHITOV, ORDER YOU TO STOP!

'Accused of thievery by the irate owners of Hotel Yalta, Dante defended his integrity in time-honoured outlaw tradition.
'He ran like hell.' — BRIGANDS OF THE EMPIRE, BY MARIA BERIA.
Nikolai Dante
HEY!
IT'S MY PARTY AND I'LL FLY IF I WANT TO!
THE GENTLEMAN THIEF PART 4

WHO INVITED YOU ANYWAY, LARDASS!?

TURGENEV TO LORD KONIGSBERG. DANTE IS IN THE GAMBLING SECTOR.
ORDERS?

HOLD HIM UNTIL CAPTAIN ARBATOV AND I ARRIVE.
BUT DON'T HURT HIM TOO BADLY— THAT'LL BE OUR PLEASURE.
SCRIPT ROBBIE MORRISON
ART SIMON FRASER
COLOURS ALISON KIRKPATRICK
LETTERS ANNIE PARKHOUSE

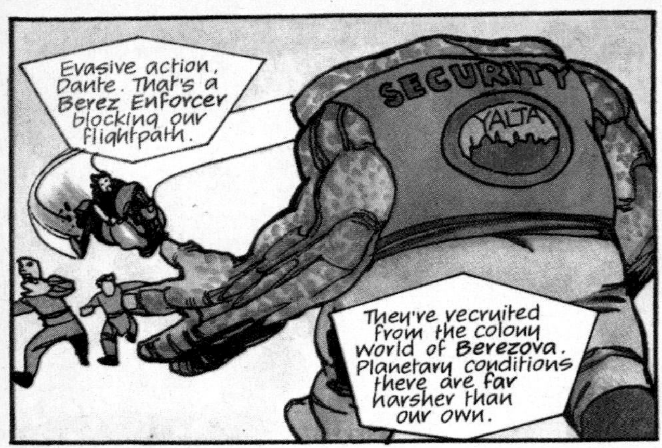
Evasive action, Dante. That's a Berez Enforcer blocking our flightpath.
SECURITY
YALTA
They're recruited from the colony world of Berezova. Planetary conditions there are far harsher than our own.

Due to Earth's lower gravity, the Enforcers' strength and power are incredible.
YEAH!? SO'S OUR SPEED!

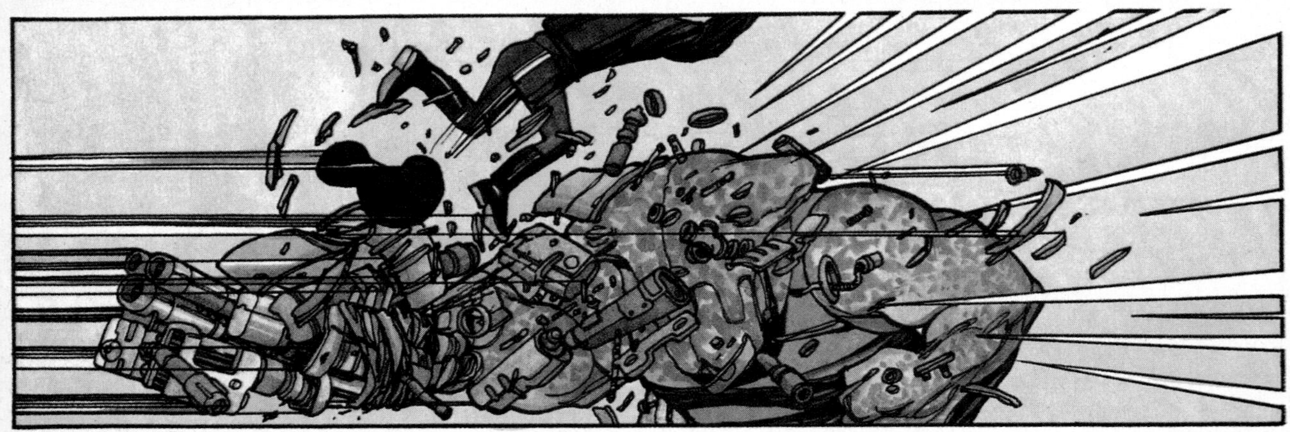

And so is your overconfidence...
FUOCO!

YOU'D NEED A TANK TO STOP A BEREZ ENFORCER, THIEF.
THIEF?

DANTE!?

LET'S BRING THE HOUSE DOWN ON HIM, CREST!

STEALING KISSES FROM THE WRONG PEOPLE AGAIN, NIKOLAI DANTE?
SOMETHING LIKE THAT, COUNTESSA.

HEY! WHOA!
YOU KNEW IT WAS ME IN YOUR BEDCHAMBER?
OF COURSE.
A WOMAN OF MY BREEDING CAN TELL A LOT FROM A KISS.

DANTE!
YOU'RE NOT DOING TOO WELL, ENFORCER.

HERE!
TRY YOUR LUCK ON THE ROULETTE WHEEL!

HUHH!?

HHHGGLLPPP!

MY SINCEREST APOLOGIES FOR THIS DISTURBANCE, COUNTESSA DE WINTER. WHERE DID DANTE GO?
THERE. TO THE YALTA'S COMMAND CENTRE.
PLOOO

C'MON. C'MON.

PALMPRINT ACCEPTED. RETINAL SCAN ACCEPTED.
IDENTITY CONFIRMED.

WHY WOULD ANYONE WHO CAN'T PAY THEIR BILL BE LUNATIC ENOUGH TO ENTER THE COMMAND CENTRE?

WHAT KEPT YOU, GENTLEMEN!?
IF YOU WISH TO CHECK, I BELIEVE YOU'LL FIND MY BILL HAS BEEN PAID. IN FULL.

AND I BELIEVE IT'S TIME YOU PAID FOR YOUR CRIMES!
IN FULL!

CAPTAIN, I'M THE ONLY VICTIM OF THE GENTLEMAN THIEF HERE.
I'M THE ONLY ONE WHO CAN PROPERLY IDENTIFY HIM.
HOW!?

I'M AFRAID DANTE'S NOT YOUR THIEF — HIS TONGUE IS TOO SHORT AND HE DROOLS TOO MUCH.
A LADY OF THE COUNTESSA'S BREEDING CAN TELL A LOT FROM A KISS.

LORD KONIGSBERG, THE BILL FOR DANTE'S PARTY HAS BEEN SETTLED — BY ORDER OF THE TSAR. PAYMENT AUTHORISED BY CAPTAIN ARBATOV.
IMPOSSIBLE!
DANTE HACKED INTO YOUR SYSTEM!

ISN'T THE FINANCIAL SECURITY OF THE YALTA IMPREGNABLE?
YOUR GUESTS WOULD SOON DESERT YOU IF THEY THOUGHT THEIR ACCOUNTS COULD FALL VICTIM TO FRAUD OR HACKING.
YEAH, THERE'S NO ONE TIGHTER WITH MONEY THAN THE LORDS AND LADIES OF THE THIEVES' WORLD.

UH, OF COURSE OUR UH, SECURITY IS IMPREGNABLE.
ENFORCERS, SUBDUE ARBATOV— THE TSAR WON'T BE PLEASED TO LEARN HOW YOU'VE SQUANDERED HIS REGIMENT'S MONEY, CAPTAIN.

DAMN YOU, DANTE— GGLLRRKK!
THIS PARTY'S OVER, COUNTESSA.
MAYBE WE SHOULD GO TO MY SUITE AND START ONE OF OUR—

'COUNTESSA?'

DAMN!

AND I THOUGHT SHE WAS AFTER MY BODY...

FOR EVERY GENTLEMAN THIEF, THERE'S A LADY WHO'LL STEAL HIS HEART

THE END

NEXT PROG ▷ THE FULL DANTE!

THE FULL DANTE

Script: Robbie Morrison

Art: Charlie Adlard

Letters: Annie Parkhouse

Originally published in *2000 AD* Prog 1071

Nikolai Dante
When venturing out in public, a Russian aristocrat should provide an impeccable role model for lesser imperial subjects, conducting himself with dignity and decorum at all times.
THE FULL DANTE
BULLSEYES!
Unfortunately, the words 'dignity' and 'decorum' rarely feature in the vocabulary of my 'master' Nikolai Dante, as proven by his playboy half-brother Andreas Romanov's recent suggestion of a quiet evening out...
Two days, 19 brawls, 19 wrecked taverns, seven successful seductions (31 unsuccessful), and incalculable amounts of vodka later...
STOP SQUIRMING, MAN!
IF YOU AND YOUR COMRADES HADN'T STARTED A FIGHT WITH US AND WRECKED ALL THE FURNITURE, YOU WOULDN'T BE IN THIS POSITION.
BOJEMOI!
THE YEAR OF THE TSAR 2666. SHCHERBAKOV, DRINKING CAPITAL (DISPUTED) OF THE RUSSIAN EMPIRE.
ANDREAS!
THERE'S AN ARMY— hic!—A SEA OF WOMEN SURGING PAST US. SURELY IT'S OUR HELL-RAISING DUTY TO DROWN AMONGST THEM?
ROBBIE MORRISON
CHARLIE ADLARD
ANNIE PARKHOUSE

'The Cossacks! Stallions Of The Steppes! The sexiest dance troupe to ever strut their sculptured wares before the noblewomen of the Empire!'
—***ONE OF THE MORE MODEST TURNS OF PHRASE FROM THE COSSACKS' TOUR PROGRAMME.***

GET 'EM OUT FOR THE LADIES!

GET 'EM OFF!

LADIES! LADIES! LADIES!

WHY WORK YOURSELVES INTO A LATHER OVER THESE —*hic!*— PREENING, PUMPED-UP POSEURS WHEN YOU'VE GOT A ***PRIME*** SPECIMEN OF THE IMPERIAL ARISTOCRACY IN YOUR MIDST?

YOU!? YOU'RE EVERYTHING THAT'S WRONG WITH THE ARISTOCRACY—AN ARROGANT, INBRED, VODKA-SWILLING, CIGAR-PUFFING SLOB!
OUR BODIES ARE TEMPLES, WORKS OF ART. VANITY PLAYS NO PART IN OUR APPEARANCE!

But if you don't stop hogging our limelight, we'll kill you.

I'M TOO—hic!—COOL TO KILL...
PUT THAT IN YOUR POUCH AND SMOKE IT!

LADIES!
THE NAME'S NANTE —hic!—DIKOLAI NANTE. IF YOU WANT TO TEST THE FIRMNESS OF RUSSIAN MANHOOD, FEEL FREE TO FONDLE MINE.

OUFFF!

Dante, in your present state of inebriation, your crude, dirty-fighting techniques may prove less than effective.
EVEN TOTALLY SMASHED, CREST...

THERE'S NO WAY I'M GETTING MY HEAD POUNDED IN BY A POSSE OF POSING POUCHES!

AHHHH!

AOWW! MY MOUSTACHE! AOWW!

AOWWWWWWW!

KBUFF!

AFTER THAT, WHAT COULD I POSSIBLY DO FOR AN ENCORE?

GET 'EM OFF AND GET 'EM OUT!
WE PAID TO MAKE FUN OF SOME DANGLY BITS, AND BY VLADIMIR'S BEARD, WE BETTER SEE THEM!

DIAVOLO!
IF THERE'S ONE THING MORE DANGEROUS THAN A WOMAN SCORNED, IT'S A WHOLE ARMY OF THEM SCORNED. BUT IF YOU CAN'T BEAT THEM...
LIGHTS...
MUSIC...
ACTION!
I'm beginning to get the impression that you're enjoying this sordid show a little more than you should be, Dante...
SPLUTCH!

Tut, tut, tut...
NO SELF-CONTROL— THAT'S THE TROUBLE WITH AMATEURS.
DON'T ALL FAINT AT ONCE, LADIES...

THE FULL DANTE'S STILL TO COME!

THWUMPH!

I believe you require a longer shaft to properly execute the pole vault, Dante.

Tell me...

Does losing your clothes and being forced to return home in a pair of animal-pube underpants normally constitute a quiet evening out? Another man's pants at that...
I'M TELLING YOU, CREST, IF YOU WEREN'T BONDED TO ME...

THE END

MOSCOW DUELLISTS

Script: Robbie Morrison

Art: Simon Fraser

Colors: Alison Kirkpatrick

Letters: Annie Parkhouse

Originally published in *2000 AD* Progs 1072-1075

THE YEAR OF THE TSAR 2666.
THE IMPERIAL PALACE OF TSAR VLADIMIR THE CONQUEROR.

IT'S TRULY A *PLEASURE* TO HAVE THE IMPERIAL DYNASTIES AS OUR GUESTS ONCE MORE, ISN'T IT, *JENA*?

Nikolai Dante

MOSCOW DUELLISTS PART 1

YES, FATHER, *ESPECIALLY* THE HOUSE OF *ROMANOV*.

SCRIPT ROBBIE MORRISON
ART SIMON FRASER
COLOURS ALISON KIRKPATRICK
LETTERS ANNIE PARKHOUSE

THIS HISTORIC GATHERING IS TO MARK THE UNVEILING OF A *MONUMENT* TO ALL THE *GLORIES* OF THE EMPIRE AND TO THE *UNQUESTIONED* AUTHORITY OF *MY* RULE.

BEHOLD, MY SUBJECTS!
THE THIRTEENTH WONDER OF THE EMPIRE!
NEW MOSCOW!
THE FACE OF THE EMPIRE!
THE VISAGE OF POWER!
SURVEYING THE WORLDS AND GALAXIES OF THE EMPIRE—MERCIFUL AND BENEVOLENT TO THOSE WHO LOVE AND HONOUR ME.

ТИТАНИК
MERCILESS AND MALEVOLENT TO ANY WHO DARE OPPOSE ME.
AWESOME!
MAGNIFICENT!
THE WORK OF ART TO END ALL OTHER ARTISTIC ENDEAVOURS!
LOOKS AS THOUGH HE'S GOT SNOTTERS DRIBBLING FROM HIS NOSE.

THIS IS AN OUTRAGE, VLADIMIR!
YOU RAISED THE TRIBUTE YOU DEMAND FROM THE DYNASTIES TO BUILD THIS EGOMANIACAL MONSTROSITY!?

SUCH SYMBOLS OF POWER—ICONS, IF YOU WILL—ARE IMPORTANT FOR THE MORALE OF MY SUBJECTS.
RULING AN EMPIRE IS NO CASUAL AFFAIR, DMITRI. YOU OF ALL PEOPLE SHOULD KNOW THAT.
THE FAMILY ROMANOV LOST THE FIRST EMPIRE AND PLUNGED US INTO CENTURIES OF CHAOS.

SURELY AN INCREASE IN TRIBUTE IS A SMALL PRICE TO PAY FOR KEEPING THE PRESENT EMPIRE SAFE IN MY CAPABLE HANDS.

AHH, THE OSTENTATIOUS GRANDEUR OF ARISTOCRATIC LIFE. YOU MUST FIND IT ALL RATHER OVERWHELMING, LITTLE BROTHER.
STRAIT-LACED AND BORE·THE·PANTS·OFF·YOU·DULL, KONSTANTIN. BRING ON THE BEER AND THE DANCING GIRLS...

LET'S MINGLE, NIKOLAI. I'LL FAMILIARISE YOU WITH SOME OF THE OTHER GUESTS—I KNOW EVERYONE.
YOU GET AROUND THEN, NASTASIA?

THE HOUSE OF RASPUTIN, A.K.A. THE DEVIL'S MARTYRS. A FANATICUL CULT DEVOTED TO OUR FAMILY'S OLD NEMESIS GRIGORI RASPUTIN.
THE HIGHER RANKS REPUTEDLY POSSESS PSIONIC POWERS.

I'VE BRUSHED BRISTLES WITH THEM BEFORE...

'MIKHAIL DERIABIN, ELECTED HEAD OF THE HOUSE OF BOLSHOI, THE LARGEST MEDIA AND ARTS CONGLOMERATE IN THE EMPIRE...
'AND HIS LOVER, THE FIREBIRD, BALLERINA QUEEN OF THE DANSE MACABRE.'

'THE BLACK DRAGONS, GOVERNORS OF THE DARK OCEAN AND THE MANY THOUSANDS OF ISLAND COMMUNITIES WITHIN IT.'
'A TREACHEROUS ALLIANCE OF YAKUZA SOCIETIES, CURRENTLY CHAIRED, SOMEWHAT MURDEROUSLY, BY THE SAGAWA CLAN.'

'REPRESENTATIVES FROM THE HOUSES OF NUMA, TANTOR AND KONG, CONTROLLERS OF THE FORMER AFRICAN CONTINENT.'
'EVOLVED FROM ENDANGERED SPECIES SEEDED WITH HUMAN INTELLIGENCE TO PROMOTE THEIR SURVIVAL, THEY WIPED OUT THEIR HUMAN AGGRESSORS AND ASSUMED POWER!

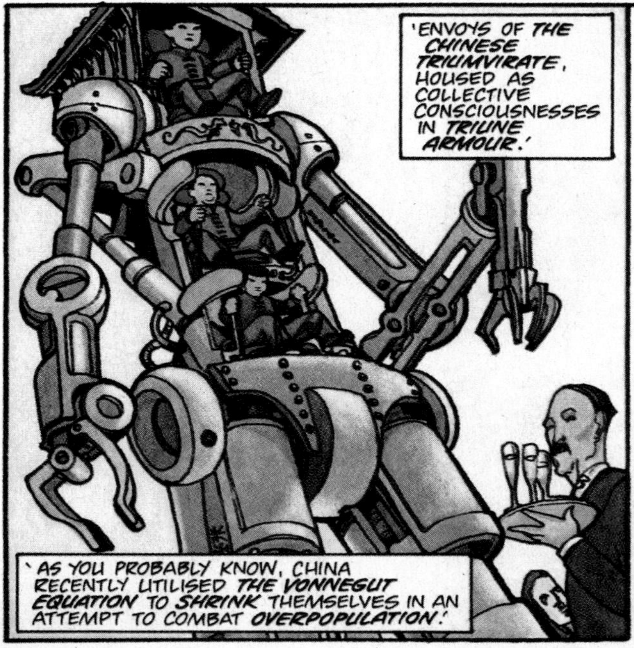
'ENVOYS OF THE CHINESE TRIUMVIRATE, HOUSED AS COLLECTIVE CONSCIOUSNESSES IN TRIUNE ARMOUR.'
'AS YOU PROBABLY KNOW, CHINA RECENTLY UTILISED THE VONNEGUT EQUATION TO SHRINK THEMSELVES IN AN ATTEMPT TO COMBAT OVERPOPULATION!'

CAIUS ZACHAROVITCH, THE FENCING MASTER.
HE WAS GIVEN CONTROL OF THE KARAZIN'S LANDS WHEN THE TSAR OUTLAWED THEM.

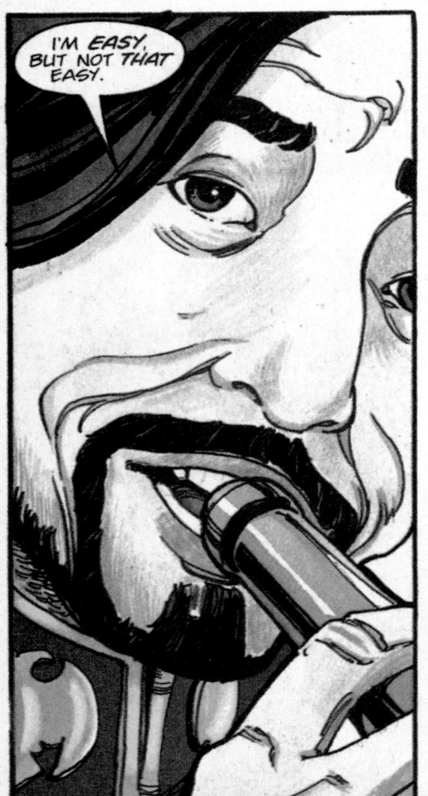

NEXT PROG ⏩ THE DANGER OF DIRTY THOUGHTS!

'The breathtaking unveiling of New Moscow was somewhat overshadowed by the celebrations that followed.

Nikolai Dante

Moscow Duellists Part 2

'In particular, the audacious behaviour of a man fast becoming a permanent fixture in the scandal pages of this publication...

"...Nikolai Dante, illegitimate sibling of the Romanov Dynasty!' — THE IMPERIAL TIMES.

Assassinations and duels are de rigueur amongst the noble houses at these events. Give no one an excuse to challenge you.

RELAX, CREST, I'LL BE THE EPITOME OF AN IMPERIAL GENTLEMAN.

SCRIPT ROBBIE MORRISON
ART SIMON FRASER
COLOURS ALISON KIRKPATRICK
LETTERS ANNIE PARKHOUSE

If you're a gentleman, then chivalry has finally curled up and died.

WHAT'S THE WORLD COMING TO WHEN A MAN CAN'T EVEN THINK IN PEACE?
I DIDN'T KNOW YOU HAD INTELLECTUAL LEANINGS, NIKOLAI. I PRESUMED YOUR MIND WAS BLISSFULLY FREE OF ALL THOUGHT.

NOT ALL THOUGHT, JENA.
THE DIRTY ONES ARE AIMED STRAIGHT AT YOU...

YOU FILTHY, ARROGANT, SEWER-BRED RAT!
LANGUAGE LIKE THAT COULD ONLY COME FROM A MIND AT LEAST AS DIRTY AS MINE...

'COURSE, THEY DO SAY GREAT MINDS THINK ALIKE.
AND I THINK THEY SHOULD COME TOGETHER TOO... FOR PASSIONATE DEBATE.

Y'KNOW, YOU'LL PUT SOMEONE'S EYE OUT WITH THAT.
WHY, MILADY, WHAT ARE YOU TALKING ABOUT?

YOUR SWORD, THIEF...
AAOOWW

THERE, THERE, YOU'LL BE ALRIGHT.
DO YOU WANT PRINCESS JENA TO KISS IT BETTER?
CLUMSY BARBARIAN! I AM NOT A CHILD!

THE ROMANOV PIG HAS BLINDED NUMBER 336!
HEY! WHOA!
IT WAS AN ACCIDENT!

CRUSH HIS LOFTY ARROGANCE!
CUT HIM DOWN TO SIZE!
HHAAA!!
KKIYEEEH!!

THERE'S NO WAY I'M GETTING DONE IN BY THE SEVEN DWARVES!

WWAAAHHH!

STRIKE ONE FOR THE MAN IN ROMANOV RED.
TIME FOR ANOTHER DRINK, I THINK...

?
HEY, VIKTOR.
HOW'S IT GOING?

THAT, SIRRR, WAS THE LAST BANANA! AND IT HAD MY NAME ON IT!
HUH?

HAS THE WHOLE WORLD GONE MAD OR SOMETHING!?
I'M BEING HASSLED ABOUT A BANANA BY A TALKING APE!?

BANANAS ARE OF GRRREAT IMPORRRTANCE TO THE HOUSE OF KONG.
I DEMAND SATISFACTION THRRROUGH--

TRIAL BY COMBAT!? UH UH!
YOU WANT A FIGHT, FUZZY, LET'S GO FOR IT! HERE AND NOW, YOU AND ME!

WHO DARES?
WHOA!

HALT!
THERE SHALL BE NO BLOODSHED IN THE IMPERIAL PALACE. ALL DISPUTES WILL BE SETTLED THROUGH OFFICIALLY-SANCTIONED DUELS.
I'LL GLADLY RRRIP HIM LIMB FROM LIMB IN YOURRR NAME, TSARRR VLADIMIRRR.

!!!
DANTE ALREADY HAS A PRIOR ENGAGEMENT— WITH ME.
HE PLAYED PINBALL WITH THE ENVOYS OF THE CHINESE TRIUMVIRATE! WE DEMAND SATISFACTION THROUGH TRIAL BY COMBAT!
!!
Bojemoi... it never rains but it pours...

EXCELLENT!
THE DUELS SHALL FORM A TOURNAMENT, THE BLOOD OF WHICH WILL CHRISTEN MY NEW CITY.
OF COURSE, YOUNG DANTE...

WHILE I'M GRATEFUL FOR THE ENTERTAINMENT OPPORTUNITY YOU'VE CREATED, I CAN HARDLY IGNORE THE DISHONOURABLE WAY IN WHICH YOU'VE REPAID MY HOSPITALITY.

CAIUS ZACHAROVITCH. YOU SHALL FIGHT DANTE ON BEHALF OF MYSELF AND THE EMPIRE.
THE BOY HASN'T INSULTED ME, SIRE. THE RULES OF DUELLING STATE THAT PERSONAL HONOUR--

HE HAS INSULTED ME, CAIUS. AND AS YOU SAID, YOUR SWORD IS MINE. I HOPE YOU INTEND TO HONOUR YOUR WORD.

YES, TSAR VLADIMIR.

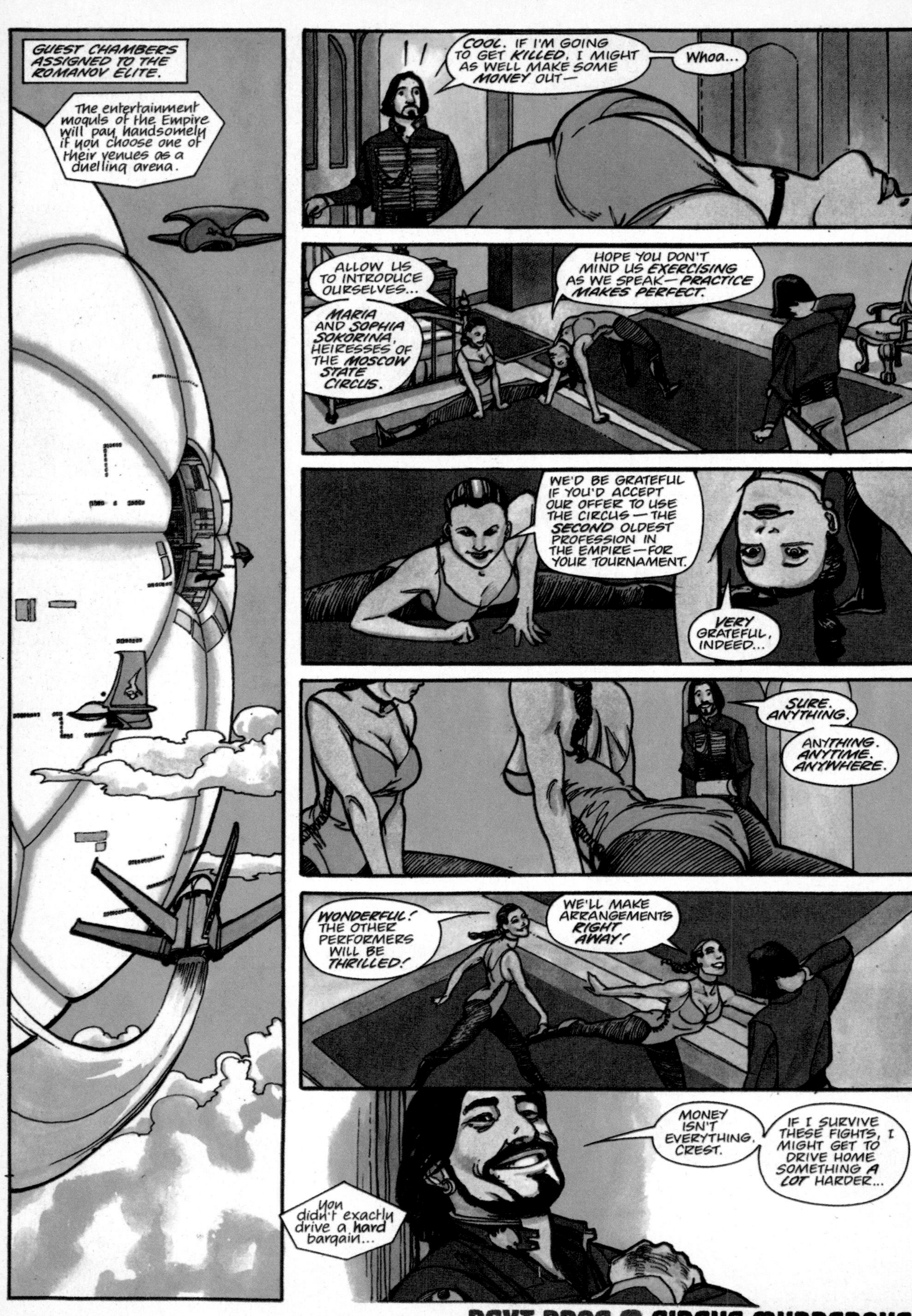
GUEST CHAMBERS ASSIGNED TO THE ROMANOV ELITE.
The entertainment moguls of the Empire will pay handsomely if you choose one of their venues as a duelling arena.
COOL. IF I'M GOING TO GET KILLED, I MIGHT AS WELL MAKE SOME MONEY OUT—
Whoa...
ALLOW US TO INTRODUCE OURSELVES...
MARIA AND SOPHIA SOKORINA, HEIRESSES OF THE MOSCOW STATE CIRCUS.
HOPE YOU DON'T MIND US EXERCISING AS WE SPEAK— PRACTICE MAKES PERFECT.
WE'D BE GRATEFUL IF YOU'D ACCEPT OUR OFFER TO USE THE CIRCUS — THE SECOND OLDEST PROFESSION IN THE EMPIRE — FOR YOUR TOURNAMENT.
VERY GRATEFUL, INDEED...
SURE. ANYTHING.
ANYTHING. ANYTIME. ANYWHERE.
WONDERFUL! THE OTHER PERFORMERS WILL BE THRILLED!
WE'LL MAKE ARRANGEMENTS RIGHT AWAY!
You didn't exactly drive a hard bargain...
MONEY ISN'T EVERYTHING, CREST.
IF I SURVIVE THESE FIGHTS, I MIGHT GET TO DRIVE HOME SOMETHING A LOT HARDER...
NEXT PROG • CIRCUS MURDEROUS!

Dante

NEW MOSCOW IMPERIAL CIRCUS.

MOSCOW DUELLISTS PART 3

YEAH, WE ENDED UP WITH OUR TONGUES DOWN EACH OTHER'S THROATS...
AND IT'S WAY PAST TIME FOR A REMATCH.

GGGNNPH!

Y'KNOW, CREST, I THINK SHE'S FINALLY BEGINNING TO FALL FOR ME.
And how do you arrive at that conclusion?

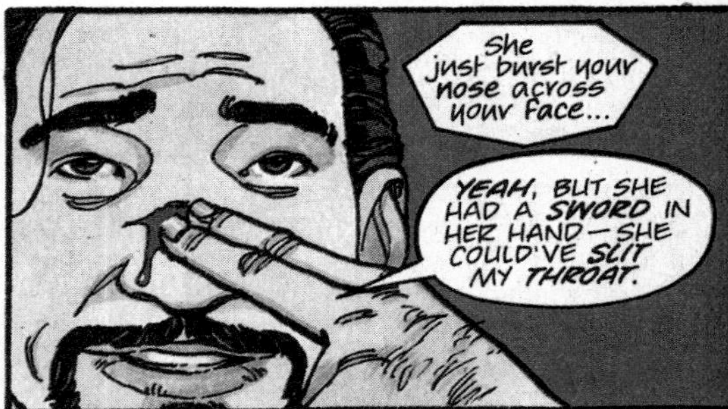
She just burst your nose across your face...
YEAH, BUT SHE HAD A SWORD IN HER HAND—SHE COULD'VE SLIT MY THROAT.

MILORDS AND LADIES!
THE IMPERIAL CIRCUS IS PLEASED TO BRING YOU A DUELLING TOURNAMENT TO CELEBRATE THE OPENING OF NEW MOSCOW AND THE RULE OF VLADIMIR THE CONQUEROR!

NIKOLAI DANTE, ACCUSED OF ALMOST EVERY INSULT UNDER THE SUN, WILL DEFEND HIS HONOUR AGAINST FOUR ASSAILANTS...
INQUISITOR KLYASKA OF THE DEVIL'S MARTYRS, NUMBERS 333, 336 AND 369 OF THE CHINESE TRIUMVIRATE.
GENERAL URKO OF THE HOUSE OF KONG AND CAIUS ZACHAROVITCH, THE FENCING MASTER!

COMBATANTS--
ENTER THE ARENA AND DO YOUR DUTY!

UH, THE DUEL STARTS AS SOON AS WE STEP INTO THE RING?
OF COURSE, BOY!
DIDN'T YOU EVEN FAMILIARISE YOURSELF WITH THE RULES?

UUURRKK!

DIDN'T READ MY MIND THAT TIME, DID YOU?

NEXT!

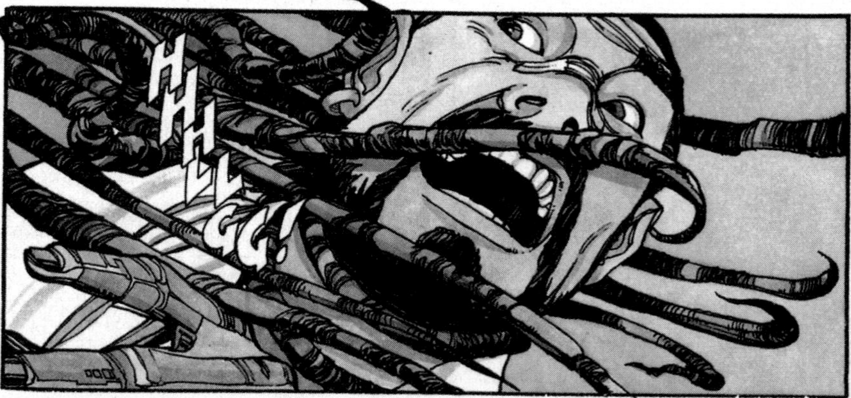

HHHLGG!

YOU DON'T DESERVE THE HONOUR OF FAIR COMBAT, ROMANOV!
WE'LL WHIP YOU LIKE THE TREACHEROUS DOG YOU ARE!
Weapons analysis: Triune Armour, which coalesces its weavers' minds into a collective consciousness.

DIAVOLO!

No, you stunted fools...
You've thrown him backstage!

WHOA...
TALK ABOUT SKIDMARKS!

SLICE HIM IN THREE!
WE'LL BE PROMOTED FOR THIS!
NO LONGER SHALL WE SKULK IN THE LOW HUNDREDS AS 333, 336 AND 339...

THWACK!
WE'LL STAND TALL IN THE THOUSANDS AS 999, 1008 AND—
WHAT...!?

KERRUMP!

Alfredo Marconi And His Acrobatic Elephants!
BOJEMOI!
DIO MIO!
CAN'T A MAN TRAIN HIS ANIMALS IN PEACE!?

NEXT PROG ● FIRST BLOOD!

'The noble tradition of duelling reached its nadir during the infamous New Moscow tournament, when Nikolai Dante was challenged by warriors from four noble houses.'

Nikolai Dante

Moscow Duellists Part 4

SCRIPT ROBBIE MORRISON
ART SIMON FRASER
COLOURS ALISON KIRKPATRICK
LETTERS ANNIE PARKHOUSE

'Choice of weapons was elephantine, to say the least...' — *A HISTORY OF DUELLING, IVAN GERASSIM.*

HAHAHAHAHA!

NEW MOSCOW IMPERIAL CIRCUS.

THIS IS *FARCICAL*.

MY SUBJECTS PAID TO CHEER THE *DEATH* OF *NIKOLAI DANTE*, NOT TO YELL *ABUSE* AT AN *EMPTY RING*.

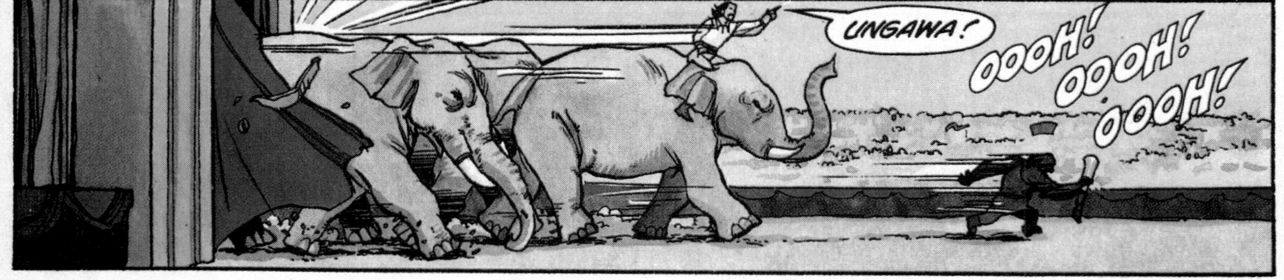

CAIUS! CAIUS! CAIUS!
LISTEN TO THEM.
THE ARISTOCRACY, THE IMPERIAL NOBILITY...

SCREAMING FOR BLOOD, CHEERING ON THEIR PET KILLERS.
WHAT?
WASN'T IT ALWAYS LIKE THIS?
MAYBE.

MAYBE I JUST NEVER REALISED...

I PLEDGE TO CONDUCT MYSELF WITH HONOUR AND DUEL TO FIRST BLOOD IN THE NAME OF TSAR VLADIMIR THE CONQUEROR.

I'LL DEFEND MYSELF WITH PASSION AND PANACHE AND PROVE WHAT THE LADIES OF THE THIEVES' WORLD ALREADY KNOW — THAT I REALLY AM TOO COOL TO KILL.

'COURSE, IF I DON'T, I HOPE YOU'LL ACCEPT A SHALLOW CUT ON THE PINKIE AS EVIDENCE OF FIRST BLOOD...

EN GARDE, SIR.
UH, YEAH, RIGHT...
EN GARDE!

Diavolo...
NOT ANOTHER STRIPTEASE AT SWORDPOINT!

THE BLADE IS AN ARTIST'S WEAPON, DANTE. IT MUST BE WIELDED WITH PINPOINT ACCURACY...

AND RAZOR-SHARP REFLEXES.
WHOA! NOT THE BEARD, MAN! THAT'S LOW...

YOU SWING A SWORD LIKE AN EXECUTIONER'S AXE. LIKE SOME BRAWLING BARBARIAN DRUNK.

FENCING ISN'T ABOUT STRENGTH OR POWER OR AGGRESSION, BOY, IT'S ABOUT CONTROL.

GGRRAAA!
REMAIN COMPOSED AT ALL TIMES. NEVER LOSE YOUR TEMPER.

DON'T LUNGE AND THRUST LIKE SOME SEX-STARVED OAF IN A BORDELLO. KEEP YOUR BALANCE, MAINTAIN YOUR POISE...

AND ALWAYS, ALWAYS KEEP YOUR GUARD UP.

FUOCO...
GO ON. DO IT.

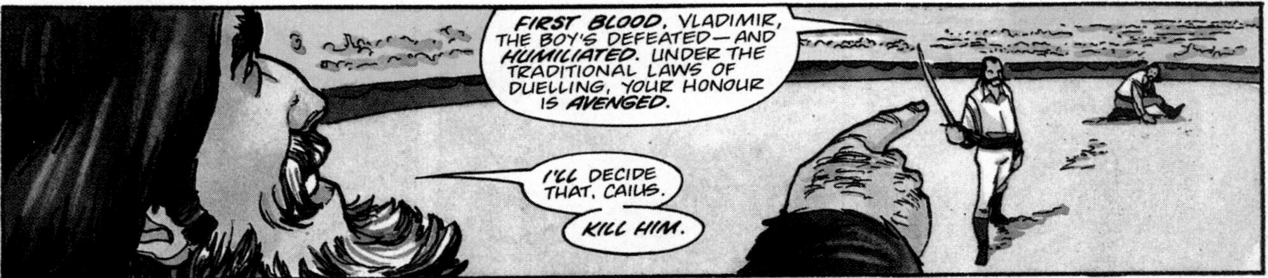
FIRST BLOOD, VLADIMIR, THE BOY'S DEFEATED—AND HUMILIATED. UNDER THE TRADITIONAL LAWS OF DUELLING, YOUR HONOUR IS AVENGED.
I'LL DECIDE THAT, CAIUS.
KILL HIM.

I'VE KILLED ENOUGH FOR YOU, VLADIMIR, AND I'M BEGINNING TO DOUBT THAT YOU AND YOUR EMPIRE ARE WORTH KILLING FOR.
MAYBE THEY NEVER WERE, MAYBE I WAS JUST A FOOL...

THEN I HOPE YOUR NEW-FOUND PRINCIPLES ARE WORTH DYING FOR, CAIUS.
PYRE!

CAIUS!
JENA, MY LOVE. COMPOSE YOURSELF.
NOW.

CAIUS...
JENA TOLD ME YOU WERE LIKE A FATHER TO HER. THE EMPIRE WOULD BE A BETTER PLACE IF YOU HAD BEEN.
KEEP YOUR GUARD UP...
...boy...
'I have no words. My voice is in my sword...' —SHAKESPEARE, MACBETH.
THE IMPERIAL PALACE.
DANTE!
Nikolai...
GUEST CHAMBERS ASSIGNED TO THE ROMANOV ELITE.
JENA! WHAT'RE YOU DOING HERE?
I...THIS ISN'T EASY FOR ME TO SAY...
I CAME TO THANK YOU FOR WHAT YOU SAID TO CAIUS IN THE ARENA. IT... WAS NICE...
PROBABLY THE MOST DECENT THING YOU'VE--
HEH he HEH!
Uh, JENA...
YOU'VE MET MARIA AND SOPHIA SOKORINA? HEIRESSES TO THE IMPERIAL CIRCUS...

JENA!
Ahh, fuoco...

HEIRESSES IN YOUR BED AND PRINCESSES AT YOUR DOOR...
WHAT KIND OF MAN ARE YOU, NIKOLAI DANTE?
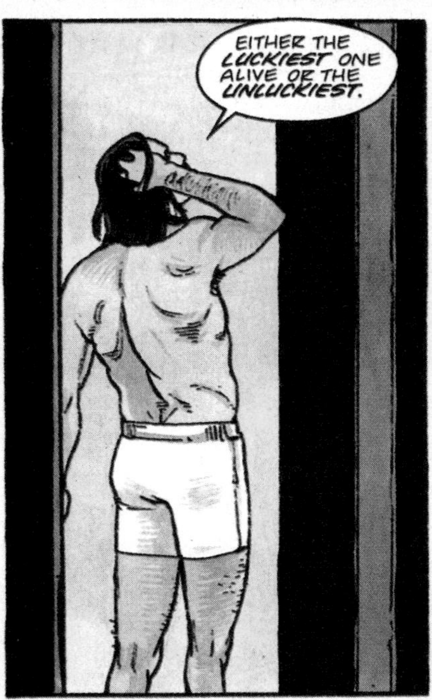
EITHER THE LUCKIEST ONE ALIVE OR THE UNLUCKIEST.

WHAT THE HELL...
AS YOU SAY IN THE CIRCUS, THE SHOW MUST GO ON!

GET READY FOR SOME LOVING!
I'M COMING IN LIKE FLYNN!

COME BACK HERE YOU UNGRATEFUL BEASTS!
12
THE END

Dante

THE GULAG APOCALYPTIC

Script: Robbie Morrison

Art: Henry Flint

Letters: Annie Parkhouse

Originally published in *2000 AD* Progs 1079-1082

'The measure of civilisation in a society is judged by the treatment of its prisoners...' — DOSTOYEVSKY.
THE YEAR OF THE TSAR 2667.
SAMOVAR, GULAG WORLD OF THE ROMANOV DYNASTY. THE HARSHEST PRISON COLONY IN THE EMPIRE.
ATTENTION, PRISONERS! NO TALKING. KEEP YOUR EYES FIXED AHEAD, YOUR HANDS BEHIND YOUR BACKS.
ONE STEP OUT OF LINE IS AN ATTEMPT TO ESCAPE. CONVOY ESCORTS HAVE ORDERS TO SHOOT AND SLASH WITHOUT WARNING.
NOW! QUICK MARCH!

NIKOLAI DANTE

THE GULAG APOCALYPTIC

PART 1

STARSHIP ANDREI TARKOVSKY TO SAMOVAR COMMAND. REQUEST PERMISSION TO BEGIN PLANETARY APPROACH.

AWW, COME ON...

SCRIPT ROBBIE MORRISON
ART HENRY FLINT
LETTERS ANNIE PARKHOUSE

YOU **MUST** BE IMPRESSED BY NOW.

LOOK! ONE HAND!
AND IF I CAN DO THIS, JUST IMAGINE WHAT **OTHER** POSITIONS I CAN GET INTO.

COME ON. WE'RE NEARLY THERE...
AT LEAST TELL ME YOUR NAME.
KHARA.
NICE NAME...

STRANGE...
I WAS THINKING EXACTLY THE SAME OF YOU.

I'LL, UH, MAKE SURE EVERYTHING'S SECURE BACK IN YOUR SUITE, JUST IN CASE SOMEONE ATTACKS FROM THERE.

A WISE STRATEGY. AND IN CASE YOU FORGET, MY RIFLE WILL BE WITHIN EASY REACH.
NAKED AND DRIPPING OR FULLY CLOTHED, I'M AN EXCELLENT SHOT.

'NAKED AND DRIPPING!' BOJEMOI...
CREST? X-RAY VISION ISN'T AMONG THE CAPABILITIES YOU CAN GIVE ME, IS IT?
No. Not for the ungentlemanly purpose you have in mind.

OH, NIKOLAI!
AREN'T YOU SUSPICIOUS THAT YOUR ESCORTING ME MIGHT BE AN ELABORATE PLOY FOR THE ROMANOV DYNASTY TO RID THEMSELVES OF YOUR EMBARRASSING PRESENCE?

NO ONE RETURNS FROM SAMOVAR, ISN'T THAT WHAT THEY SAY?

THE WINTER PALACE OF THE ROMANOV DYNASTY. THREE DAYS AGO.
AS WELL AS BEING OUR MAIN GULAG, SAMOVAR IS OUR RICHEST SOURCE OF MINERALS AND FUEL.
YOU WILL ESCORT OUR VISITING ALLY HERE TO SAMOVAR COMMAND. IT'S VITAL THAT HER IDENTITY REMAINS A SECRET TO ALL CONCERNED WITH THE FLIGHT, INCLUDING YOURSELF.
WHAT YOU DON'T KNOW CAN'T HURT YOU— OR US.
ONCE YOU'VE DELIVERED HER SAFELY, YOU'LL REMAIN THERE, FAMILIARISING YOURSELF WITH OUR OFFWORLD HOLDINGS, UNTIL WE SEND FOR YOU.
AND WHEN WILL THAT BE?
IT'LL BE WHEN WE SEND FOR YOU.
IT'S JUST I'VE GOT A THING ABOUT PRISONS, LORD DMITRI— EVERY WOMAN I'VE EVER KNOWN TOLD ME I'D END UP IN ONE.
'FACT, MOST OF THEM SAID THEY'D HAPPILY DO THE LOCKING UP.
AND I LIKE IT HERE AT THE PALACE.
I MEAN, IT'LL BE COLD WAY OUT THERE.
OH, POOR BOY...
DON'T WORRY. I'LL BUY YOU A GREATCOAT.

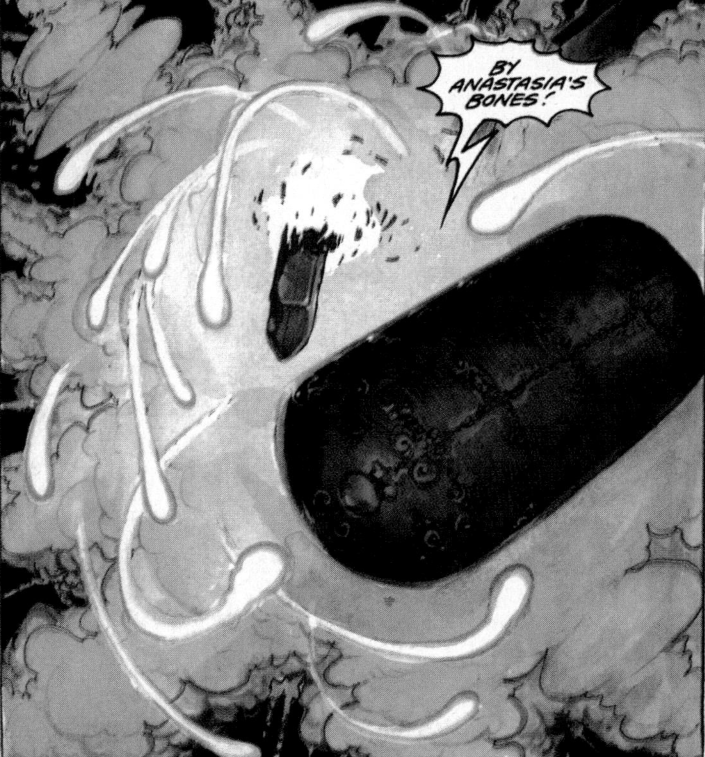

NEXT PROG ⏩ COMPROMISING POSITIONS!

'When it comes to being in the wrong place at the wrong time, there's not a man alive can touch me.'
'The explosion that disabled the Samovar prison colony brought down our ship, killing the crew.'
— NIKOLAI DANTE, BRIEFING THE ROMANOV DYNASTY ON THE SAMOVAR INCIDENT.
NIKOLAI DANTE
PART 2 THE GULAG APOCALYPTIC
SCRIPT ROBBIE MORRISON
ART HENRY FLINT
LETTERS ANNIE PARKHOUSE
'Luckily, I had a soft landing.'
nuhhh...
WHAT!?
HUH?
TALK ABOUT COMPROMISING POSITIONS.
HOPE YOU DON'T THINK I ENGINEERED THE CRASH JUST TO SET THIS UP?
NO, NIKOLAI.
I WOULDN'T CREDIT YOU WITH THAT MUCH INTELLIGENCE.

CREW OF THE ANDREI TARKOVSKY!
LAY DOWN YOUR WEAPONS AND SURRENDER YOURSELVES IN THE NAME OF THE ROMANOV DYNASTY!
WHO!?
THE ISOLATORS. THE GULAG'S ANDROID ENFORCERS.
MAYBE YOU SHOULD IDENTIFY YOURSELF BEFORE THEY RECOGNISE YOUR CRIMINAL TENDENCIES AND MISTAKE YOU FOR A NEW ARRIVAL.
THE NAME'S DANTE. NIKOLAI DANTE.
AS FAR AS YOU'RE CONCERNED, I AM THE ROMANOV DYNASTY, SO START SHOWING SOME RESPECT OR I'LL ISOLATE YOUR HEAD FROM YOUR BODY.
WAS THAT DOMINANT ENOUGH FOR YOU?
Dante! The Isolators aren't responding to my communications!
WHOA! CREST!?
An unidentified intelligence has infiltrated their command network —they are no longer under Romanov control!
KHARA!
GET OUT OF HERE! I'LL TAKE CARE OF THEM!
My hero...
SLASH-SHXXX!
KRZZ-KKK!

CREST, YOU'RE THE SUPER-COOL BATTLE COMPUTER. DO SOMETHING!
REGAIN CONTROL OR BLAST THEIR CIRCUITS TO KINGDOM COME!
Don't you think I'm trying?
TRY HARDER!!
BDAMM! BDAMM! BDAMM! BDAMM! BDAMM!
NICE MOVE, CREST.
I HAD EVERY CONFIDENCE IN YOUR ABILITIES.
Unlike you, Dante, I cannot tell a lie — I had nothing to do with their destruction.
WITH RESPECT, NIKOLAI...
YOU'RE SUPPOSED TO BE MY BODYGUARD?

WE'LL HEAD FOR SAMOVAR COMMAND—WHAT'S LEFT OF IT—AND HAVE YOUR WEAPONS CREST ANALYSE THE SITUATION.
SURE THING—AFTER SEEING YOUR SHOOTING, I'M NOT GOING TO ARGUE.
QUITE A PISTOL YOU'RE PACKING.

THE HUNTSMAN 5000 A SELF-RELIANT, MULTI-PURPOSE WEAPONS SYSTEM, CODED SPECIFICALLY TO MY GENEPRINT.
AMMUNITION IS CREATED INTERNALLY AND REPLENISHED AUTOMATICALLY—NO NEED TO LOAD OR RELOAD.

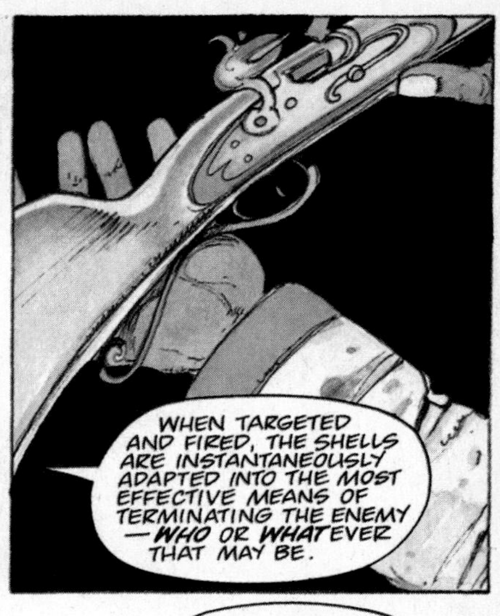
WHEN TARGETED AND FIRED, THE SHELLS ARE INSTANTANEOUSLY ADAPTED INTO THE MOST EFFECTIVE MEANS OF TERMINATING THE ENEMY—WHO OR WHATEVER THAT MAY BE.

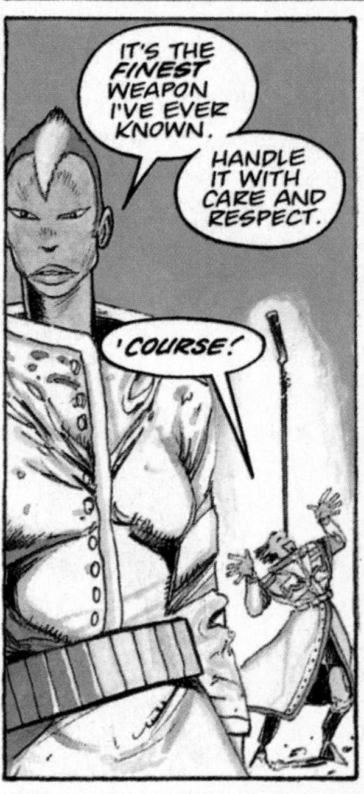
IT'S THE FINEST WEAPON I'VE EVER KNOWN.
HANDLE IT WITH CARE AND RESPECT.
'COURSE!

WONDERFUL DESIGN. YOUR EYES JUST FLOW TOWARDS THE TARGET.
BEAUTIFUL CURVES AND CONTOURS...

WHAT?
NOTHING!
PICK A TARGET AND I'LL SHOW YOU HOW ACCURATELY I SHOOT MY LOAD.

I'D LOVE TO SEE YOU TRY.
IT'S CODED TO MY GENEPRINT—IF ANYONE ELSE FIRES IT, THE BULLET REVERSES TRAJECTORY AND USES THEM FOR TARGET PRACTICE.

Scanning Samovar Command...
No survivors amongst the Romanov forces stationed here, though the prisoners remain secure in their cells. The computer network is still under enemy control.
Stay alert, Dante.
ALERT, YEAH. RIGHT.
SO, WHERE'D YOU GET THE GUN, KHARA? I'VE NEVER SEEN ANYTHING LIKE IT, AND I'VE BEEN AROUND A BIT.
NOT THAT MUCH YOU HAVEN'T.
BOJEMOI!
WHAT THE HELL IS THAT?
REMEMBER WHAT YOUR FATHER SAID?
WHAT YOU DON'T KNOW CAN'T HURT YOU.
WHAT I DON'T KNOW CAN PROBABLY KILL ME A LOT QUICKER THAN WHAT I DO KNOW!
CREST, WHAT IS IT?
There is no information in my databanks, but I believe it leads to where I was created...
You're kidding.

NEXT PROG ⏩ NO-ONE RETURNS FROM SAMOVAR!

'Under attack from an enemy who had singlehandedly seized control of the Samovar prison colony and decimated the troops stationed there...
'I defended myself and the lovely Lady Khara with the courage and determination one would expect from the Hero of Rudinshtein.'
NIKOLAI DANTE, EMBELLISHING HIS ROLE IN THE SAMOVAR INCIDENT TO THE ROMANOV DYNASTY.
NIKOLAI DANTE
THE GULAG APOCALYPTIC
PART 3
YOUR CHOICE IS SIMPLE, KHARA. BECOME ONE WITH US.
OR DIE.
SCRIPT ROBBIE MORRISON
ART HENRY FLINT
LETTERS ANNIE PARKHOUSE
THE LADY'S UNDER MY PROTECTION.
YOU WANT HER, YOU HAVE TO CROSS BLADES WITH ME...
AS YOU WISH, ANIMAL.
Dante--
I KNOW, I KNOW...
EVASIVE ACTION!

DANTE! DOWN!
BZAKKK!
LIKE THE WAY I SET HIM UP TO GIVE YOU A GOOD SHOT?
SHUT UP, THIEF! THAT'S A WHITE ARMY REIVER!
HE CAN ALTER HIS CYBERNETIC STRUCTURE TO COMBAT THE EFFECTS OF MY AMMUNITION. IT'S LIKE A BATTLE OF WILLS.
SPLUT!
SPDANG!
SPANG!
I THINK WE'RE GOING TO NEED MORE WILLPOWER.
FZERKKKZZ!
HE'S NOT FOLLOWING US...
HE CONTROLS THE GULAG, HE CAN USE ANY MANNER OF MEANS TO TRACK US.
HE'S A TEKNOCRAT— HE'LL CHOOSE THE MOST LOGICAL MOMENT TO PICK US OFF.

YOU DESERVE TO KNOW THE TRUTH, NIKOLAI, EVEN IF YOU *HATE* US ALL FOR IT.
'DECADES AGO, CYBORGANIC TECHNOLOGY SIMILAR TO YOUR WEAPONS CREST WAS INTRODUCED TO MY RACE, TO FURTHER OUR EVOLUTION, TO *IMPROVE* US, BUT TECHNOLOGY DOESN'T WORK THAT WAY...
'ITS PURPOSE IS TO *ADVANCE ITSELF* — AT ANY PRICE. IT BEGAN TRANSFORMING US INTO LIFEFORMS LIKE THE REIVER, MORE CYBERNETIC THAN ORGANIC.
'OUR SOCIETY SPLIT INTO TWO FACTIONS: *THE WHITE ARMY*, WHICH EMBRACES THE MUTATIONAL PROCESS AND HAS SWORN TO WIPE OUT THE WEAKNESSES OF THE FLESH; AND *THE RED GUARD*, WHO FIGHT TO PRESERVE OUR '*HUMANITY*'.

'THE ENERGY VORTEX YOU SAW IS A BRIDGE BETWEEN MY UNIVERSE AND YOURS, CAUSED BY SOME COSMIC UPHEAVAL. THE REIVER MUST HAVE INFILTRATED THE FORTRESS WE BUILT AROUND IT.
'THROUGH THE BRIDGE, THE RED GUARD AND THE ROMANOV DYNASTY FORMED AN ALLIANCE. IN RETURN FOR CREST TECHNOLOGY, THE ROMANOVS SUPPLY US WITH UNTAINTED GENETIC MATERIAL TO COMBAT THE ONSLAUGHT OF CYBORGANIC MUTATION.
'GULAG INMATES WHO HAVE GROWN TOO WEAK TO WORK SAMOVAR ANY LONGER.'
No one returns from Samovar...

SAMOVAR OIL PRODUCTION PLATFORMS.
THE REIVER MUST'VE BROKEN THE PRODUCTION PROGRAMME WHEN HE COMMANDEERED SAMOVAR'S COMPUTER NETWORK.
THE WELLS ARE LEAKING BADLY.
NOT THE CLEVEREST PLACE FOR US TO BE — A FIREFIGHT'LL TURN THE PLATFORM INTO AN INFERNO.
US!? NICE TO KNOW YOU'RE CONCERNED ABOUT A PIECE OF GENETIC MATERIAL LIKE ME!
THE INMATES SENT TO US WERE MURDERERS, RAPISTS--
YEAH, YEAH!
AND THIEVES WHO STOLE TO FEED THEIR FAMILIES, DISSIDENTS STUPID ENOUGH TO THINK THEY COULD CHANGE THE EMPIRE JUST BY TALKING ABOUT IT AND ANY OTHER POOR SCUMBAG WHO WASN'T COOL ENOUGH TO BE BORN INTO THE ARISTOCRACY.
MY KIND OF PEOPLE!
WHAT KIND ARE YOU!?
I'M A WAR-CHILD, WHAT THE WHITE ARMY MADE ME! I'LL DO WHATEVER I HAVE TO TO FIGHT THEM!
I DON'T HAVE TO BE PROUD OF IT!
I HOPE YOU NEVER TASTE WAR, NIKOLAI.
It's all I've ever Known.
NOTHING'S BLACK AND WHITE.
IT'S NEVER THAT EASY...
IT CAN BE, LIEUTENANT KHARA.
YOU ONLY HAVE TO BECOME ONE WITH US.

NEXT PROG ⏩ BIG BANG BOOM!

'It was the kind of reckless devil-may-care plan that only the Hero of Rudinshtein could've pulled off with the necessary style.
'Lure the cybernetic assassin who had taken control of the Samovar Gulag to an oil platform, trap him in an inferno of hellish proportions and then make a death-defying leap to the decks below.'
NIKOLAI DANTE
SCRIPT ROBBIE MORRISON
ART HENRY FLINT
LETTERS ANNIE PARKHOUSE
THE GULAG APOCALYPTIC
PART 4
WHOA!
'Fortunately, I had another soft landing.'
—NIKOLAI DANTE, WIT AND RACONTEUR (IN HIS OWN EYES), RELATING THE SAMOVAR INCIDENT TO THE ROMANOV DYNASTY.
WE KEEP ENDING UP IN THESE COMPROMISING POSITIONS...
THINK SOMEONE'S TRYING TO TELL US SOMETHING?
ANIMALS!
AAARRGH!

UUUUNNHH!
YOU WILL BE ONE OF US, LIEUTENANT KHARA!

THE WHITE ARMY WELCOMES YOU INTO ITS RANKS.
NO...
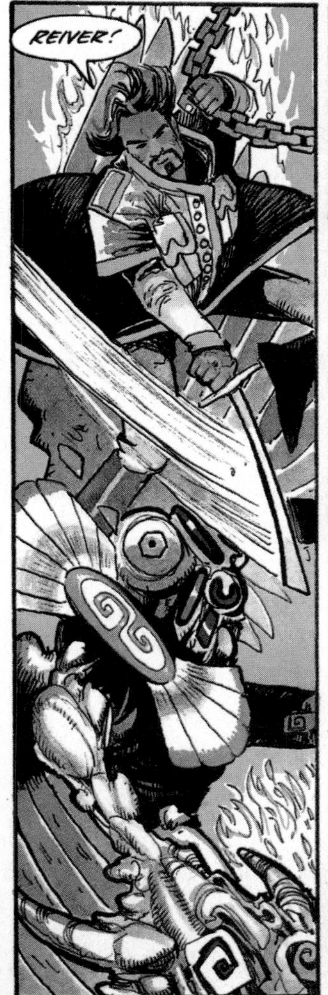
REIVER!

THE LADY'S UNDER MY PROTECTION.

YOU STILL WISH TO CROSS SWORDS WITH ME, ANIMAL?

YEAH!
CROSS THEM AND SHOVE THEM UP YOUR--

AAAAGHKK!
I WILL CRUSH YOU, ANIMAL, CRUSH ALL YOUR KIND.
YOU CAN'T CRUSH US ANY FURTHER, REIVER.
YOU, THE ROMANOVS, THE TSAR, YOU'RE ALL THE SAME.
I'M GOING TO RAISE A SEWER-BRED ARMY OF THIEVES, SEDUCTRESSES AND MURDERERS.
WE'LL FIGHT AND BOOZE AND SLEEP OUR WAY ACROSS THE UNIVERSE, BRING DOWN YOUR EMPIRE, THIS EMPIRE...
EVERY EMPIRE.
WE'LL CRUSH YOU INTO THE GUTTER, GIVE YOU A TASTE OF REALITY.
WE'LL RULE OVER YOU, SEE WHO'S WORSE...
OR IF WE'RE ALL AS BAD AS EACH OTHER.
YOUR WORDS ARE BORN OF INSANITY, BUT YOU FENCE WELL, IF NOTHING ELSE.
I HAD A GOOD TEACHER.
BEST IN THE EMPIRE.
THERE IS MORE TO WAR THAN FENCING, ANIMAL SCUM!!

THE NAME'S DANTE! NIKOLAI DANTE!
PRIZE SCUMBAG OF THE RUSSIAN EMPIRE!
EEEEEEEAAAAGH!

AND PROUD OF IT...

YOU KILLED HIM!
A WHITE ARMY REIVER, NIKOLAI! AND YOU KILLED HIM!
I TOLD YOU, LADY KHARA, I TAKE MY DUTIES AS A BODYGUARD VERY SERIOUSLY.

SPEAKING OF BODIES, WE BETTER GET SOME SHELTER BEFORE OURS START FREEZING.

Ohh, I'M SURE YOU'LL THINK UP SOME WAY OF KEEPING US WARM...

YOU HUMANS ARE SO POORLY EVOLVED.
ALL HAIRY AND UGLY.
HEY, A BIT OF ROUGH NEVER HURT ANYBODY.
A GREATCOAT.
GREAT.
YOUR REINFORCEMENTS ARE ARRIVING.
I HAVE TO GO. I'M SORRY...
THE BRIDGE WILL RETURN ME TO MY PEOPLE. I'VE REPROGRAMMED THE HUNTSMAN TO ENCODE ITSELF TO YOU. YOUR GENE-PRINT WILL AUTOMATICALLY SUPERSEDE MINE.
KEEP IT...
YOU NEED EVERYTHING YOU CAN TO HELP YOU STAY ALIVE.
STAY WITH ME...
KOLYA...
IT'S NOT AS IF WE'RE ONLY FROM DIFFERENT WORLDS OR GALAXIES — WE'RE FROM DIFFERENT DIMENSIONS.

SO?

YOU'RE A FOOL, NIKOLAI DANTE.

YEAH...
AN UGLY FOOL AT THAT.

OUR ORDERS ARE TO IMPOSE ORDER ONCE MORE AND RETURN YOU TO THE WINTER PALACE WITH ALL POSSIBLE HASTE.

ANY ADVICE ON PLANETARY CONDITIONS, LORD NIKOLAI?
ADVICE?
SURE...

DON'T EAT ANY YELLOW SNOW.
THE END

2000 AD Prog 1035: Cover by **Simon Davis**

2000 AD Prog 1039: Cover by **Simon Davis**

2000 AD Prog 1044: Cover by **Trevor Hairsine**

2000 AD Prog 1074: Cover by **Trevor Hairsine**

2000 AD Prog 1080: Cover by **Henry Flint**

Nikolai Dante portrait
by **Simon Fraser**

Early Jena Makarov sketch
by **Simon Fraser**

Robbie Morrison is one of *2000 AD*'s most popular writers, having co-created *Blackheart*, *The Bendatti Vendetta*, *Shakara*, *Shimura* and *Vanguard*, and chronicled the adventures of Judge Dredd in *2000 AD*, *Judge Dredd Megazine* and a UK national newspaper. He is also co-creator of the fan-favorite Russian rogue *Nikolai Dante*, which recently won an Eagle award for Best UK Character — beating Judge Dredd to this accolade for the first time in almost twenty years.

In the US, Morrison has written *Spider-Man's Tangled Web* for Marvel and recently completed work on a new story arc for DC/WildStorm's *The Authority*. His critically acclaimed graphic novel *White Death* has been hugely successful in both Europe and the US, and he and *White Death* artist Charlie Adlard have recently reunited for a story in DC's *Batman*.

Charlie Adlard made his debut pencilling *Judge Dredd* in the eponymous *Megazine*. Since then, he has also illustrated *Armitage* and *Judge Hershey* in the *Meg*, and *Judge Dredd*, *Nikolai Dante*, *Pulp Sci-Fi* and *Rogue Trooper* in *2000 AD*. His most recent work for the Galaxy's Greatest Comic is the official sequel to *Invasion!*, the hard-hitting *Savage*. Beyond *2000 AD*, Adlard has illustrated *Astronauts in Trouble*, *Codeflesh*, *The Establishment*, *Shadowman*, *The X-Files*, and the graphic novel *White Death*.

Simon Fraser is best known to *2000 AD* fans as the co-creator of Russian rogue Nikolai Dante, whose adventures have been a staple of the comic since his debut in 1997. Fraser is also the co-creator of *Family* in the *Judge Dredd Megazine*, and he has drawn *Judge Dredd* and *Shimura* as well. His best-known non-*2000 AD* work is *Lux & Alby: Sign On and Save the Universe*, a collaboration with Scottish post-punk author Martin Millar. Fraser is currently working on an adaptation of Richard Matheson's *Hell House* and is also writing and drawing *Lilly Mackenzie and the Mines of Charybdis*.

Henry Flint is one of the Galaxy's Greatest Comic's rising superstars. Co-creator of *Sancho Panzer* and *Shakara*, he has also lent his incredibly versatile pencils to *A.B.C. Warriors*, *Judge Dredd/Aliens*, *Bill Savage*, *Deadlock*, *Judge Dredd*, *Rogue Trooper*, *Missionary Man*, *Nemesis the Warlock*, *Nikolai Dante*, *Sinister Dexter*, *Tharg the Mighty*, *The V.C.s*, *Vector 13* and *Venus Bluegenes*. He has even written a *Tharg's Alien Invasions* strip! In addition, Flint has begun to establish himself in American comics, working on the anthology titles *AIDS Awareness*, *Ammo Armageddon* and *Monster Massacre*.